Northwest Wreck Dives

by

Scott Boyd

and

Jeff Carr

First Edition

First Published December 2008

Published by Emerald Sea Scuba, LLC.
P.O. Box 5877
Lacey, WA 98509

www.northwestwreckdives.com

ISBN: 978-0-9821510-1-3
Library of Congress Control Number: 2008908925

All photos by Scott Boyd.
All wreck maps by Jeff Carr.

Printed in Centralia, Washington State, USA.

Acknowledgements

In the preparation of this guide, several individuals went above and beyond the call of duty in providing us with help, information, and encouragement without which this book would never have happened. Foremost among those, the authors have to thank Janet Boyd. She not only put up with both Jeff and Scott for two straight years of relentless wreck diving and research (every weekend), but was also an excellent (and always available) boat captain that not only kept us safe, but fat and happy as well.

Many other individuals contributed time and knowledge to the cause including, but not limited to: John Sharps, Scott Christopher, Jeff Waugh, Eric Thornton, Zena Monji, Jeff Trembly, Roland Anderson, Mike Fitz, Mike Allen, Jessica Fichtel, Ron Akeson, Donny Richcreek, Jeff's Family, Nibbler and Eugene Skin Divers.

The authors also wish to recognize that their fascination with wreck diving started long ago while reading the grand books written by James A. Gibbs, the <u>Shipwrecks of the Pacific Coast</u> and <u>Shipwrecks off Juan de Fuca</u> and Gordon R. Newell's book, <u>Ships of the Inland Sea</u>.

We are also looking forward to finding many new wrecks in the future. We would like to encourage our readers to keep sending us those rumors, tips, and tidbits of local knowledge that sometimes will lead to the excitement and discovery of a new wreck.

Table of Contents

Appendices

**Photos of many of the wrecks listed in this book
can be found on Scott's web site at
www.boydski.com.**

Disclaimer

The authors have worked cautiously and with the best knowledge available to ensure that the information within this book is correct. No guarantee of accuracy is expressed or implied within this manuscript and it may well contain errors or information that has changed over time. The charts and maps within this book should not be used for navigation. The authors are in no way responsible for what you do with the information provided to you within this document or corollary information found on our website.

This book was written to provide information to divers of all levels. It is up to the individual diver to determine what is safe or not safe for them. Training is readily available for divers of all skill levels. We simply cannot list all of the potential issues that a diver may face and make no implication that we have.

Safe diving is your responsibility.

Stern of the Wreck Orca

Introduction

Thank you for purchasing our guide to Northwest Wrecks. It was written as a reference to assist divers in locating and safely diving the numerous wrecks that are in or near the state of Washington. There are still many new ones to be discovered. We encourage you to embrace the exploration bug that is found in all of us and to venture forth and find them. The rush that you get when you discover a new wreck is a magical thing, and we hope that this guide opens up new dive sites, new adventures, and new discoveries for you.

Please use the information in this book wisely. Good training and experience in measured steps are the key to safely enjoy the wrecks presented in this book. Some of the deep, technical wrecks are treacherous for even the most experienced divers. Heed the notes and cautions offered in the reviews and try not to be "that guy" (the one we all hear stories about).

It is important to read all the material within this book before tackling a new dive. Experience has left a few kernels of good advice scattered throughout the book.

Have fun, be safe and dive smart.

Wreck Diving Information

The information provided in this book is organized with a summary of each wreck dive presented in the following manner:

Name: The most common or historical name that we could locate for each wreck is listed. We at times had to make up our own names for those wrecks of unknown origins.

Location: The general region or area where each wreck is located. Typically this would be the nearest city or land reference.

GPS: The location of each wreck is listed using the Global Positioning System coordinates. See additional information on the next page for the reference datum and precision used.

Depth: The depths we recorded while diving the wreck are listed and are adjusted for a median tidal height.

Access: The closest entry point for shore dives or the nearest useable boat ramps for boat dives are listed.

Rating: Beginner, Intermediate, Advanced or Technical level of skill is indicated, along with the primary reason for the rating. See the glossary for our definitions of these skill levels.

Currents: The nearest current station is listed along with observed intensity of the current. See additional information on page 12 for locating the correct current station.

History: A brief overview of the background and known history of the wreck.

Dive Information: General diving information about the wreck and the dive site itself.

Notes: Additional information that may be useful when diving the wreck. Nearby additional dive sites are sometimes listed.

Cautions: Warnings and possible dangers associated with diving that particular wreck.

Global Positioning System

GPS: All of the GPS coordinates in this book utilize the WGS 84 reference datum, which is the default used today by most GPS units. These can generally be entered as waypoints directly into any modern GPS unit. All of the listed coordinates were located using one unit (Humminbird) and verified with another (Lowrance), but typographical errors do sometimes happen, so please let us know if you find an error in the book.

Many of the older coordinates that you may find are likely to have used the previous NAD 27 or NAD 83 reference and can be quite a ways off if entered directly into a modern GPS. This is especially true when utilizing information from NOAA's Automatic Wreck and Obstruction Information System (AWOIS) which is the origin for many of the wrecks in this guide.

All of the coordinates presented in the book are in the form of degrees and decimal minutes (dd° mm.mmm') which seems to be the most popular system in use. Most GPS units will internally record their waypoints in decimal degrees (dd.dddddd°), but will display them in whatever form you wish.

GPS conversion instructions can be found in the appendices if you need to convert the coordinates listed to decimal degrees or degrees, minutes, and seconds.

All of the positions given in this book are WAAS corrected and should be accurate to within the visibility range of a diver in cold water.

Anchoring

When anchoring near a wreck, divers should strive to not damage the wreck with their anchor. Good anchoring techniques will make for a safe, enjoyable dive and will preserve the wrecks for others to enjoy.

In order to safely anchor a boat, you need to choose appropriate ground tackle. This will typically mean having more than one anchor system for the various types of wrecks that you dive. It is never okay to drop an anchor when there is any chance of a diver below you. This is especially important when approaching a dive site that has another boat already anchored over the wreck.

Anchoring Techniques:

- Drop: Get near the wreck and drop your anchor. (Please don't do this on a fragile wreck.)

- Drop and navigate: Drop your anchor close enough to easily navigate to the wreck and back. A reel or a spool of line is a good tool to make navigation back to the anchor line easy.

- Drag and snag: Drop your anchor to one side of the wreck and gently pull it into the wreckage with the boat. (This can easily damage a fragile wreck so should only be used on large steel wrecks.)

- Shot line: Drop a small weight or bag of chain and a float. Keep the boat off of the line, then put your divers in up current of the buoy and let them drift into it to descend down the line.

- Diver placement: A diver can be put in the water with a line and lift bag. The diver can place the line on the wreck and then float the bag for the boat to attach to.

Other Anchoring Considerations:

Scope: Have enough scope to keep your anchor in place. A 3 to 1 ratio (or more) is recommended; i.e., if you are in 50 feet of water, put out 150 feet or more of line.

Line choice: Small line is hard on your hands, so try a line big enough to get a good grip. This is also less likely to chafe through on wreckage. Nylon anchor lines are much better than either Dacron or Polypropylene lines.

Line marks: Mark your anchor line so you know how much you are deploying. Inexpensive rode markers are available at marine suppliers that can easily be inserted into the line.

Attachments: Make sure you secure the attachments on all parts of your anchor system. All shackle pins should be moused or secured with a tie wrap.

Currents

The location of the closest NOAA current station that is applicable for each wreck is listed with the summary information for each dive site. Currents and tides are very different. Divers should check current tables to know when it is safe to dive a specific wreck. They should check tide tables to know when it is safe to launch their boat at a specific ramp.

To find the predicted current for a wreck listed in this book, use your web browser and go to tidesandcurrents.noaa.gov. Select products from the top menu, then currents and min/max current predictions for the present year. From the Tidal Current Predictions page, select the state of Washington from the left menu and then the region (i.e., Puget Sound, north of the Narrows) from the next page. From the Current Stations page, select the link that matches the current station listed for the individual wrecks in this guide. If this seems like too much work, just go to northwestwreckdives.com and click on the currents link to go to the same current tables.

The web site should then dynamically create a yearly current prediction table for the station nearest to the wreck you are planning to dive. Look up the dates and times and always remember to check the water before jumping in. Many of the current predictions are very accurate, but sometimes--especially in the Straits of Juan de Fuca--we have been surprised by ripping currents during predicted slack water.

Equipment Recommendations

Lights: In the Pacific Northwest it is always a good idea to bring at least one light. If you are exploring around or inside of a wreck, you will find an HID light to be most useful. Anyone venturing into overhead diving should also consider carrying backup lights.

Cutting Tools: You should always carry a sharp knife, but when diving around all of the entanglement hazards found on a wreck, it's a good idea to have two or an extra pair of shears.

Reels and Spools: Spooling out a bit of line is a great way to make it easy to find a certain spot on a wreck (like where your anchor line is). Penetration of almost any wreck is dangerous and should only be done with the appropriate training and experience.

Surface Marker Buoy: The small inflatable surface marker buoys sold by numerous companies are nice additions to your gear. If you find something and want to return to it, you can mark the place with one of these buoys or send it to the surface on a spool. They also can be attached to your anchor as an additional aid in finding it. This is also a handy way to assist in pulling the anchor. Just add more air to it prior to ascending and it will make pulling up the anchor a breeze. Be sure not to add too much. The air will expand as it goes up and you want your anchor to stay put during your ascent.

Map: A map of the wreck is a nice thing to have with you or at least in the boat. Most of the wrecks in this book have maps showing the significant features. Bring this book along with you in the boat--it will make your friends (and the authors) happy!

Artifacts

Please try to leave the wrecks in as pristine a condition as possible so that others may enjoy them as well. One of the major reasons that the wreck diving community tends to be so secretive with wreck coordinates is the damage and theft that occurs when sites are made public. This is especially true of the historic and well preserved older wrecks like those found in Lake Washington. It is illegal to remove any items or artifacts from the aircraft in the lake or from many of the wrecks listed in this book. Someone owns the artifacts or salvage rights, so please leave items where you find them.

Notes

All distances in this book are given in feet, yards, or nautical miles. Depths are written in feet and represent the depths observed on our gauges when diving the wreck, adjusted for mean tidal height. The depths will vary considerably with different tides.

Many of the more delicate, historical, or dangerous technical wrecks have been listed with charter information rather than simply providing the coordinates. After much discussion with the wreck diving community, we felt this would be a good way to help preserve those sites and to encourage divers to make their dives on those particular wrecks via a charter boat that uses good anchoring techniques.

Many of the most impressive wrecks that we are privileged to dive will not hold up long with a lot of indifferent dive boats anchoring on top of them; nor are the deep wrecks in the middle of busy shipping lanes a safe place to be spending long deco times without a professional captain and support team on the boat.

Try some of these magnificent wrecks by contacting your local dive shop and diving with one of the local charters to see how you like them. There are a few operators (listed on our web site at northwestwreckdives.com) that specialize in wreck and technical diving charters. Alternatively, there are many groups of active wreck divers that would be happy to take you out for your first dives on some of the delicate and historic wrecks in Lake Washington. Have fun, dive safe, and enjoy the wonders that Mother Nature hides from our sight below the waves.

Maps

Please see the regional maps on the following pages to locate the general positions of the wrecks listed in this guide. The reviews can be found alphabetically by the name of the wreck. On the maps, the wrecks are listed by **name**.

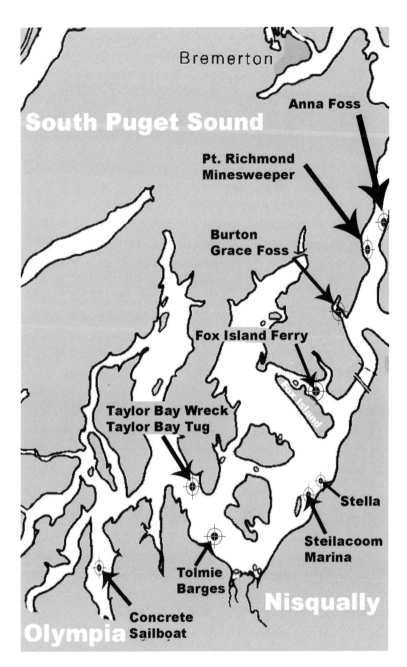

South Puget Sound Map

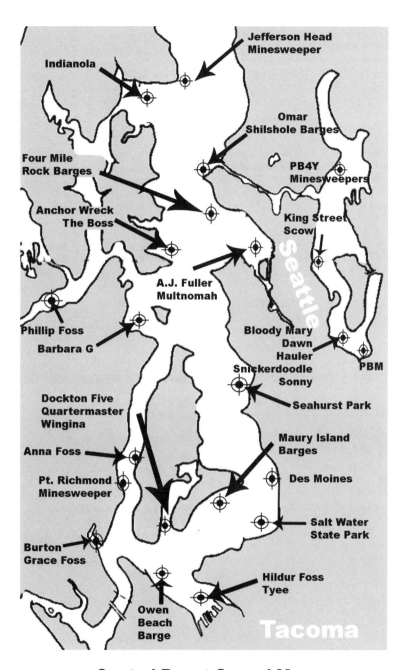

Central Puget Sound Map

17

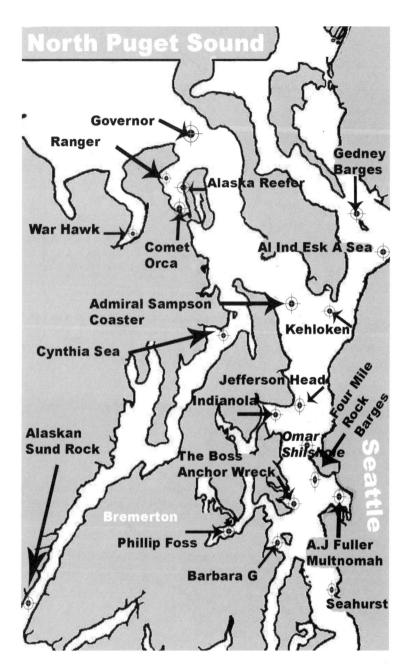

North Puget Sound

- Governor
- Ranger
- Alaska Reefer
- Gedney Barges
- War Hawk
- Comet
- Orca
- Al Ind Esk A Sea
- Admiral Sampson
- Coaster
- Kehloken
- Cynthia Sea
- Jefferson Head
- Indianola
- Four Mile Rock Barges
- Alaskan Sund Rock
- Omar Shilshole
- Seattle
- The Boss Anchor Wreck
- Bremerton
- Phillip Foss
- A.J Fuller
- Multnomah
- Barbara G
- Seahurst

North Puget Sound Map

18

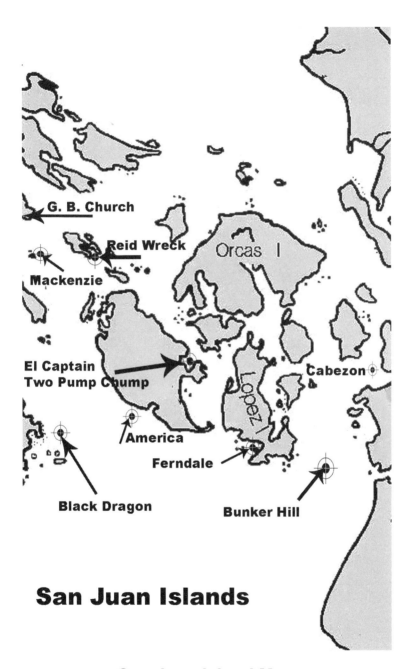

G. B. Church

Reid Wreck

Mackenzie

Orcas I

El Captain
Two Pump Chump

America

Cabezon

Lopez

Ferndale

Black Dragon

Bunker Hill

San Juan Islands

San Juan Island Map

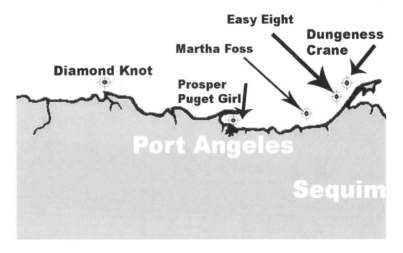

Strait of Juan de Fuca Map

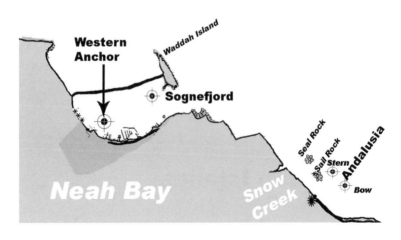

Neah Bay Map

Wreck of the Burton

Name:	**Alaska Reefer**
Location:	Walan Point, Port Townsend Bay
Position:	**48° 04.161' N 122° 44.660' W**
Depth:	**4-60'**
Access:	**Boat Dive**, ramp at Port Townsend 2.6 miles north northwest.
Rating:	**Beginner.**
Currents:	**Negligible.**

History: The 175-foot long, wood hulled *Alaska Reefer* started her life as a net tender named the *USS Pinon* (AN 66). She was built by the American Car and Foundry Co. in 1944 and served during WWII tending submarine nets in England. She was also used in Hawaii and later in Guam during the war. The ship was then sold to the Alaska Reefer Fisheries Company in 1946 and refitted as a refrigeration ship.

She was sunk just south of Walan Point on August 29, 1961, due to a fire. The firefighters thought they had the fire extinguished, but it flared up so she was beached to save some of the equipment. A salvage barge and tug were brought in and subsequently sank during the recovery effort.

Dive Information: The *Reefer* rests on her port side in shallow water near the munitions dock on Indian Island. The deeper stern section extends to a depth of 60 feet and the bow can be as shallow as 5 feet (at some tides the wreck rises slightly out of the water). Additionally, a large salvage barge can be found at a slight angle to the keel of the *Reefer*, nearly touching the hull just below the stern tube and rudder post. There is also an old tug located below the *Reefer* that sank in 1911.

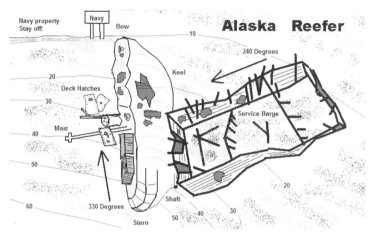

Alaska Reefer

Navy property Stay off! | Navy | Bow | 10 | 240 Degrees | Keel | 20 | Deck Hatches | 30 | Service Barge | Mast | 40 | 50 | 60 | 330 Degrees | Shaft | Stern | 20 | 30 | 40 | 50

The wooden hull of the *Reefer* is slowly rotting away, leaving the ribs of the ship exposed. Several of the holds are open, offering divers sunlit swim throughs to enjoy and explore. Lots of the old refrigeration machinery and piping are visible and bits of the diesel-electric power plant can still be seen in the engine room.

The salvage barge next to the ship has been reduced to large timbered ribs and anemones. Swimming along the keel of the *Reefer* toward the stern, you will gradually notice the skeletal remains closing in on you as the sunlight dances eerily through the dark forest of the barge's ribs.

Notes: This wreck provides excellent scenery. The currents are nearly nonexistent so you can dive this site almost anytime, but the low current also reduces the abundance of life.

Cautions: When visiting the *Alaska Reefer*, be careful not to allow your boat to swing over the forward part of the wreck. Note that the working munitions dock is a restricted navigation area, so give Walan Point a wide berth. Approach the wreck from the southwest so as not to draw the ire of the Naval Patrol boat on station at the docks.

Name:	Alaskan
Location:	Sunrise Hotel, Hoodsport
Position:	47° 24.478' N 123° 08.153' W
Depth:	20-30'
Access:	Shore Dive, entry via the dock at the Sunrise Hotel.
Rating:	Beginner.
Currents:	Negligible.

History: It appears that the wreck of the *Alaskan* is the remains of a small coastal fishing boat. There had once been a tug named the *Alaskan* in this area, but this boat does not appear to be stout enough to be a tug. Historically, the origins of the wood-hulled vessel have been lost to the staff of the Sunrise Hotel, but it makes a nice dive.

Dive Information: Just east of the dock and off to the south a few feet rests this small wreck. The rudder, fuel tanks, pipes, wires, decking and ribs are still in place about four feet off of the bottom. The *Alaskan* is a shallow, relatively safe dive and is close enough for most divers to enjoy with only a short swim from the dock.

Notes: This wreck is an interesting feature in the Hoodsport area and you will find two wee wrecks only a few feet further to the north.

Cautions: During fishing season, you may find boats running near the wreck to access the area around the fish hatchery. If you are approaching this dive site by boat, please anchor well away from the dock in deeper water and swim into the wreck.

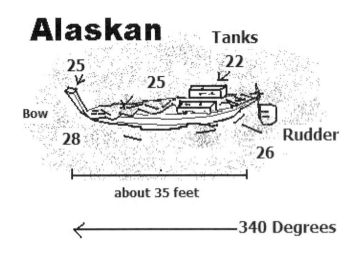

Alaskan Tanks

25

25

22

Bow

28

Rudder

26

about 35 feet

←────────────340 Degrees

Wreck of the Diamond Knot

Name:	**Al-Ind-Esk-A-Sea**
Location:	Everett, Port Gardiner
Position:	**47° 59.0336' N 122° 14.7703' W**
Depth:	**190-230'**
Access:	**Charter**, ramp in Everett 1.6 miles northeast.
Rating:	**Technical** due to depth.
Currents:	**Useless Bay**, Puget Sound.

History: The *Al-Ind-Esk-A-Sea* was built in Wisconsin and launched in May, 1945 as the private cruise ship "*Coastal Guide.*" She was renamed the *Sgt. George Peterson* and transferred to the U.S. Navy during the 1950s, spending that decade as a cargo ship. She was then placed in reserve status until being sold for commercial use in 1971.

After a series of owners, Trans-Alaska Fisheries bought the ship and renamed her *Al-Ind-Esk-A-Sea*, putting her to work as a fish processing ship in Alaska. On October 20, 1982, she was at anchor off the Port of Everett when a crew member's cutting torch ignited some insulation and set the vessel on fire. The six crew members on board escaped via the tender *Alaska Trader*.

Firefighting efforts were hampered by cyanide gas produced by the burning insulation and the danger of the 18 tons of pressurized ammonia exploding. The fireboat *Alki* eventually doused the flames on deck, but fireballs continued to burst from the lower decks through the night. The fire continued burning through the 21st, and the *Big Al* sank at 10:14 on October 22, 1982. She slipped quietly beneath the waters of Port Gardiner about a half mile offshore, where she remains to this day.

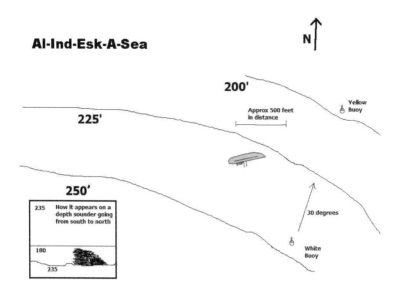

Dive Information: The *Al-Ind-Esk-A-Sea* is impressive, but a very deep wreck that is best to dive using one of the local dive charters listed at northwestwreckdives.com. The 336 foot long freighter lies on her starboard side, with her bow pointing northeast in about 230 feet of water. The port side of her large hull appears nearly level at a depth of about 180 feet because of her 50 foot beam. Her superstructure, holds, machinery, and steel hull are very much intact, which makes multiple dives a requirement if you wish to see the entire wreck.

Notes: The side of the port hull where you descend to the wreck is very flat and covered with fine silt. It looks very much like the sea floor, and more than one diver has thumbed a dive early, thinking they missed the wreck, when in fact they were on the hull.

Cautions: This is a very deep dive, and the visibility is typically poor. Technical divers should work up to dives at this depth. Stay safe and be sure to run a reel from your shot line so that you can return to the surface without having to do the not-so-fun free ascent from 200 feet.

Name:	**America**
Location:	San Juan Island, Haro Strait
Position:	**48° 29.5135' N 123° 07.1170' W**
Depth:	**20-60'**
Access:	**Boat**, Roche Harbor 8.5 miles north.
Rating:	**Intermediate** due to currents.
Currents:	**Cattle Point**, Strait of Juan de Fuca.

History: Built in Quincy, Massachusetts in 1874, the 232-foot-long bark *America* once plied the Pacific Coast trade. The graceful square-rigged vessel was built for speed, with lines similar to that of a clipper ship. She frequently raced with the *Glory of the Seas* when both were sailing the Nanaimo to California coal runs in the 1880's.

She came to an inglorious end on August 30, 1914 when she was being towed as a barge by the Steamer *Lorne* with a load of coal. She was traveling from Vancouver to Seattle en route to the British and French warships in the North Pacific. Fog had closed in and the *Lorne* towed the *America* straight onto the rocks along the western shore of San Juan Island. The *Lorne* was eventually salvaged, but the poor *America* was left to break apart on the rocks. There she lies today, nearly a century later, with only an occasional visit by divers.

The figurehead of the once proud ship was removed by Robert Moran and used as an ornament for his mansion on Orcas Island. Today, this figurehead greets visitors to the Rosario Resort on the same island.

Dive Information: The wreck is located about 1 ½ miles north of Pile Point on the west side of San Juan Island. The hull is long and narrow with one side standing about six feet off the bottom.

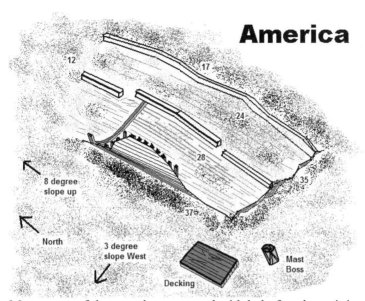

America

12

17

24

28

35

37

8 degree slope up

North

3 degree slope West

Decking

Mast Boss

Many parts of the vessel are covered with kelp fronds, so it is easy to miss the wood hull unless approaching from the north side of the wreck. At the deeper end (~ 60'), one of the old mast bosses that supported the huge masts and sails now collects sponges and critters on the bottom. The shallow end of the wreck rests in about 20 feet of water and the deeper end, some 200 feet away, is in about 60 feet. Several piles of the ship's cargo of coal are sitting inside the ribs of the hull.

Notes: There is also a very nice rocky reef just to the south and west of the deep end of the wreck. You'll find lots of interesting critters hiding in both the reef and in the *America.*

Cautions: This wreck site is very exposed to the prevailing southerly winds from the Straits of Juan de Fuca and also sees a lot of current heading up and down Haro Strait. Be sure to pick a calm day and slack water on a moderate exchange to dive this interesting bit of history. Diving in the San Juan Islands is always spectacular, and this site makes an interesting addition to several of the other nearby dive sites on the west side of the island (like Kellet Bluff or Lime Kiln Point).

29

Name:	**Anchor Wreck (aka D. Boss Cooper)**
Location:	Blakely Harbor, Bainbridge Island
Position:	**47° 35.3911' N 122° 29.5978' W**
Depth:	**80'**
Access:	**Boat Dive**, ramps at South Seattle 5 miles east or Manchester 3 miles southwest.
Rating:	**Intermediate** due to depth.
Currents:	**Mild.**

History: This small boat was once used by Lee Harvey Oswald to evade the Dallas Police on the Nile River. Then Jimmy Hoffa employed the old girl in a failed attempt to smuggle weapons onto the movie set of the Godfather III to save us all from the grief of watching it (thanks for trying Jimmy). Finally, it was accidentally beamed here from the Starship Enterprise when the transporter beam collided with D.B. Cooper in mid-air on his descent from a high-jacked airliner. Oh! All right, this boat appears to be a 1970's day cruiser and has no real history that we can find.

Dive Information: This wee wreck is about 28 feet long and sits on a sandy silt bottom. The boat is open and fairly large for its type. The old outdrive and prop are in place under the swim step. Although small and not too exciting, this wreck is near the *Boss* and might be a good place to do an extra dive.

Notes/Cautions: Not many things to worry about here, just depth and remember to navigate south if you can't find the anchor line on your trip back to the surface. Many thanks to Eric Thornton for all of his hard work researching the disappearance of D.B. Cooper and leading us to this wreck.

Anchor Wreck

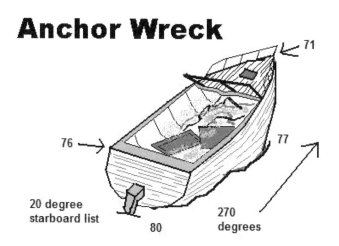

71

76 →

77

20 degree
starboard list

80

270
degrees

Anchoring

When anchoring a boat on any dive site, it is always a good idea to descend to your anchor to insure that it is secure and not in danger of chafing, slipping, or falling into deeper water. You can make adjustments to its placement and set the anchor if needed.

It is also a very good idea to take an exact depth measurement so that when you return, you will know at precisely what depth to find it.

Boat Setup

Having an organized boat/vehicle is important. Weight bags, small bins, mask pouches, and a system where everyone puts their gear in a certain place will save you a ton of headaches. Having to dig through gear piles in large bags and sorting out whose weights are whose is time consuming and invites a chance to miss out on a dive.

Name:	Andalusia

Location: Neah Bay, off of Snow Creek Resort

Positions: 48° 21.513' N   124° 32.032' W (Bow)
48° 21.633' N   124° 32.179' W (Stern)

Depth: 30-50'

Access: **Boat Dive**, ramps at Snow Creek ½ mile southwest or Neah Bay, 3 miles west.

Rating: **Intermediate** due to current and surge.

Currents: **Very Strong – West Entrance de Fuca Strait.**

History: The 7,700 ton, Panamanian-flagged tramp streamer *Andalusia* was west bound in the Strait of Juan de Fuca with a cargo of 5 million board feet of lumber from British Columbia. Captain George Lemos was soundly sleeping in his bed when he was awakened at 4:25 AM on November 4th, 1949 with word that there was fire in the engine room. Fearing for the lives of his crew, the captain turned south and headed for a nice looking beach about 3 miles east of Neah Bay.

Unfortunately, the freighter never reached the beach, as it grounded very hard about ½ mile offshore on the rocky reef out in front of what is now the Snow Creek Resort.   The crew managed to put out the fire in about ninety minutes and the USCG light tender *Fir* showed up and removed seventeen members of the crew.

The *Andalusia* was perched on a jagged reef and had taken on an extreme list, but Captain Lemos and nine crewmen stayed on board to keep the pumps running. Eventually, seven powerful tugs were secured to the freighter and pulled with everything they had. Unfortunately, they could not pull the doomed ship off of the rocks.

Four days later gale force winds struck and the captain and remaining crew were removed. Then on November 9th the pounding ocean waves won their battle with the hull of the ship as the *Andalusia* broke in two and the aft section sank near Sail Rock. Eventually, Mother Nature won the battle with the forward section of the hull, and she too slid beneath the waves.

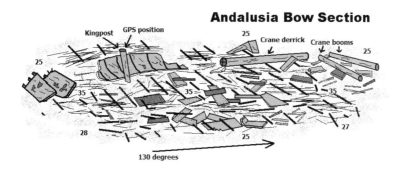

Andalusia Bow Section

48° 21.513' N   124° 32.032' W (Bow)

Dive Information: Relentless pounding by storms has flattened much of the wreckage, which is huge. Locating the wreck with a fish finder is difficult due to the rocky reefs surrounding the *Andalusia*. These are the typical ridged rock walls found in and around Neah Bay. Both sections of the wreck are against a rock wall, so differentiating between rock and steel is tough to do with a depth finder.

The twin boilers in the stern section are immense and are easy to locate (you can't miss them) just north of the position given. Near the boilers you will find the smokestack and the huge round fantail house. Several large kingposts still stand upright and the derrick and cargo booms can be found over by the rock wall to the east.

The northeast side of the once massive hull of the forward section stands proud along with a huge kingpost (where we took our GPS position). There is quite a bit of the lumber sitting in the cargo hold of the forward section, and a massive crane derrick and booms are lying along the southeast side of the wreck.

Andalusia Aft Section

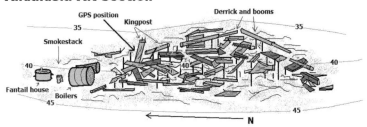

48° 21.633' N   124° 32.179' W (Stern)

Notes: The 410-foot *Andalusia* displaced 16,000 tons, nearly twice the tonnage of the *Diamond Knot*. She was built in Alameda, California, during 1918 and commissioned as the *USS Volunteer* (ID 3242). She was sold to Lykes Brothers Steamship Co. in 1937 and worked for a decade as the *SS Volunteer*. In 1948, she was sold to Transatlantica of Panama and renamed *Andalusia* before being wrecked one year later.

A salvage company used explosives to flatten the stern section of the wreckage after removing the propellers and the condensers. A large chain was then dragged through the area to clear the channel for boat traffic.

Cautions: The currents in this part of the Strait can get downright wicked. Plan your dive around slack water and keep a qualified driver in the boat to pick up anybody that gets blown off the wreck. Any significant swell coming from the Pacific Ocean will make this dive very uncomfortable due to the shallow depths and surge. There is some small boat and fishing traffic coming out of Snow Creek, so fly a dive flag and have a great time on an immense and shallow wreck.

Bathroom stops

One of the hassles of being suited up, especially if you are adhering to the hydration mantra, is taking a leak. This is especially tough on women. However, there are a few products on the market that are little known but are very helpful. Or so I am told.

One of my dive buddies, Zena (who is a Gynecologist), had a relief zipper installed in her suit that is in the same location as on the men's suits. She then uses a female urinary device which allows her to relieve herself while standing.

The *SheWee*, *Travel Mate*, *Freschette*, *Whiz Plus* and others are the brand names for these devices. A google search will lead you to the right place.

She finds them easy to use and a real lifesaver. However, these devices, although being very convenient and functional, do take quite a bit of practice before being able to write your name legibly in the snow. Or so I am told.

Maintain your Boat

Maintain your boat like it is the vehicle that will take you to a great place and then rescue you from certain disaster, because that is exactly what it will do.

Have it professionally cared for each year, adhering to maintenance schedules. Then go hang out at a busy boat ramp for a couple of hours of entertainment. The people who don't do maintenance are obvious. You see them at the boat ramps a lot--they are the ones whose motors won't start.

Name:	**Anna Foss**
Location:	Vashon Island, Colvos Passage
Position:	**47° 24.177' N 122° 31.448' W**
Depth:	**25'**
Access:	**Boat Dive**, ramp at Gig Harbor 6 miles south southwest.
Rating:	**Beginner.**
Currents:	90 minutes before **Tacoma Narrows North.**

History: The wreck of the *Anna Foss* tug is located in Colvos Passage (on the west side of Vashon Island) ¼ mile north-northeast (NNE) of Sandford Point. The wreck had once been visible at extremely low tides and can be spotted from the surface even in moderate visibility. The sixty-eight foot steam tug was built in 1907 and was originally named the *Vigilant* by the Wallace Tugboat Company of Tacoma. After going through several owners, she was converted to diesel power by Cascade Tug and then purchased through bankruptcy in 1933 by Foss Towing and renamed the *Anna Foss*. After 35 years of faithful service, she was sold and anchored at her present location for conversion.

The fifty-nine ton *Anna Foss* sank on September 16, 1969 due to general neglect and is now rapidly deteriorating. The 300 HP Enterprise engine and several salvage pontoons can be seen in and around the wreckage.

Dive Information: With a depth of only 25 feet and a site that is well protected from current, this makes a pleasant second dive after Sunrise, Dalco, or the *Richmond Minesweeper*. The wreck stands at least ten feet tall off of the bottom and much of the hull is still intact. The rudder and steering quadrant lie near the stern quarter (south end) of the wreck and are easily recognizable.

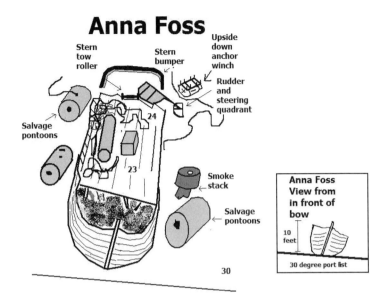

Anna Foss

Stern tow roller

Stern bumper

Upside down anchor winch

Rudder and steering quadrant

Salvage pontoons

24

23

Salvage pontoons

Smoke stack

30

Anna Foss View from in front of bow

10 feet

30 degree port list

Notes: The smoke stack sits just off the port side next to one of the salvage pontoons. Also, be sure to check the areas below the hull--especially in the front--which often house many warbonnets, gunnels, helmet crabs and other unusual creatures. This wreck is listed in the AWOIS database under the original vessel name "*Vigilant*." The location of this wreck is charted, but with the "PA" symbol which indicates Position Approximate. The charted symbol is about one-tenth of a mile west of the tug's actual location.

Cautions: There can be a lot of boat traffic and the occasional jellyfish floating along in Colvos Passage. Be sure to display a dive flag and enjoy your dive on this old wood-hulled tug. The bay containing the *Anna Foss* seems to be a magnet for flotsam and other floating debris, so approach slowly and do be careful with those inflatable boats.

Name:	**Atlantic City Barges**
Location:	Lake Washington, Atlantic City
Positions:	**47° 31.4398' N 122° 14.9918' W (PA-d3)**
	47° 31.5267' N 122° 15.0645' W (Hauled)
Depth:	**100-120'**
Access:	**Boat Dive**, ramps at Atlantic City ½ mile west or Coulon Park, 2.5 miles southeast.
Rating:	**Advanced** due to depth and visibility.
Currents:	**None.**

History: Little is known about the history of the *Hauled Barge* or the *PA-d3 Barge*. Both are located close to several other wrecks that were scuttled just off of the Atlantic City boat ramp. Prior to the level of the lake being lowered for the ship canal, there had been a working shipyard located behind the boat ramp. This is most likely the source of many of the wrecked vessels in this area.

The *Hauled Barge* has a wood hull that is located in 105 feet of water. It is not far from the wreck of the *Hauler*, which is where the name came from. This utility barge is about 45 feet long and 15 feet wide. The steel-hulled *PA-d3 Barge* is located 600 feet further south in 110 feet of water and has the letters "PA-d3" written on the stern.

Dive Information: The *Hauled Barge* sits off the bottom with a starboard list and the keel at the stern has an interesting shape that is worth a look. Of course, one look is all you might get, as the first inconsiderate person down there can easily kick up the silt enough to reduce the already low visibility to zero.

The *PA-d3 Barge* has three open compartments with wood plank flooring that once hauled coal or lumber across the lake. One end of the barge is pointy shaped, and it looks as though there once might have been some sort of mast and keel board attached to the wreck that allowed the barge to take advantage of any favorable winds.

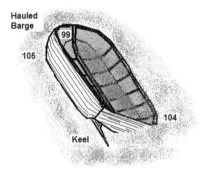

Notes: Like all of the Lake Washington dives, this wreck typically has very poor visibility coupled with lots of silt and little or no surface light. These dives are not for everyone, but are interesting little bits of history tucked away on the bottom of the lake.

Cautions: These wrecks are deep and dark enough that an inexperienced diver could easily get into trouble by running out of "no decompression time" and losing the up-line back to the boat. The barges make great training dives for technical divers as it takes just over ten minutes at these depths to accumulate a decompression obligation.

Lake Washington is very busy in the summer and the visibility is usually at its worst due to algal blooms. Most of the wrecks are best to dive in the fall or spring when there are fewer boats around. Do keep a qualified driver in the boat, and display both a dive flag and the large blue Alpha flag that is required by law.

Name:	**Barbara G**
Location:	Harper Fishing Pier, Puget Sound
Position:	**47° 31.3796' N 122° 31.0562' W**
Depth:	**30'**
Access:	**Shore Dive**, Harper Fishing Pier.
Rating:	**Beginner.**
Currents:	**Blake Island.**

History: The *Barbara G* is a really nice, shallow wreck dive located just off the end of the Harper Fishing Pier (an old Ferry Dock). The 65-foot long wood-hulled fishing boat sank during the Inauguration Day storm on January 20th, 1993. A navigation line has been run from the cluster of pilings off the end of the fishing pier to the wreck of the *Barbara G* to help shore divers locate her easily.

Dive Information: Shore access to this site is via a small two or three car parking lot next to the pier. Scramble down the rock wall and swim out past the end of the pier to the cluster of pilings (Dolphins). Follow the line about 100 feet north to the *Barbara G* which sits in only thirty feet of water. There is also another very small sailboat located a bit closer to the pilings.

Because this site is so shallow, there is plenty of light and the visibility around the fishing pier is generally good. There are also other good sites in the area, so make it a day and hit two or three wrecks.

The rudder and steering quadrant remain standing in place on the wreckage and rockfish and nudibranchs can be found hiding among the rotting ribs of the wood hull. The mast and crow's nest have fallen over onto the bottom and bits and pieces of the boat's rigging can be found scattered about. An old toilet sits below some steel combing looking like it is ready for use.

Barbara G

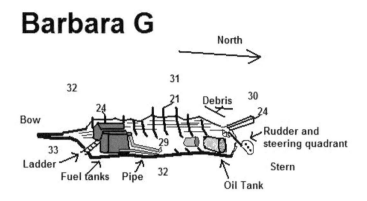

Two large steel fuel tanks sit forlornly in the hold of the *Barbara G*, playing host to colorful critters. Those familiar with fishing boats will recognize plumbing, holding tanks, winches and blocks that are visible in the mud.

Notes: It is a long swim of about 500 feet out to the end of the Harper Fishing Pier from shore. Be sure to pace yourself, descend next to the dolphins and follow the rope out to both the *Barbara G* and the small sailboat wreck at this popular dive site. Of course, if you have access to a boat, save yourself the long surface swim. Launch at the first-class, free ramp at Manchester and have a pleasant dive on this wonderful site.

Cautions: Not much in the way of hazards at this site unless you slip on a rock getting into and out of the water or incur the wrath of one of the home owners near the site for parking inappropriately. I suppose you could do something boneheaded like forgetting to tie off the anchor line only to find the boat adrift when you surface. I'm pretty sure most of you are much smarter than that.

Name:	**Black Dragon**
Location:	Northeast of Johnstone Reef, Victoria, B.C.
Position:	**48° 29.155' N 123° 15.314' W**
Depth:	**120-160'**
Access:	**Boat Dive**, Technical Dive Charter.
Rating:	**Technical.**
Currents:	**Very Strong, Discovery Island** in Haro Strait.

History: Originally named the *Hueg Ryong Pusan No. 705* prior to its dark days of smuggling immigrants, the *Black Dragon* was used in the Korean drift-net fishery off the China Coast. In 1999 the vessel made its way to the Canadian coastline where the crew forced 130 or more immigrants to swim ashore on Kunghit Island in the Queen Charlottes. In 2000 the confiscated hulk was sold to the Artificial Reef Society for $1 to be used later as an artificial reef. Eventually it was resold and was left in Mayne Bay where it "accidentally" sank in 120 feet of water.

The *Black Dragon* was raised in December 2003 and was under tow to a ship breaker in Ladysmith, B.C. when it sank for good one mile northeast of Johnstone Reef, not far from Victoria.

Dive Information: The '*Dragon*' is a shallow tech dive. Its depth is just over the recreational diving limit of 130 feet. Depth is not the demon here, it is the current, which is often unpredictable and vicious. The water can be calm at the surface and howling once you get near the bottom.

The wreck lies upright on the sandy bottom with its stern pointing in a southerly direction. This large and rusting hulk is dark, but an easy wreck to navigate around if you have an idea of the layout prior to your dive.

Black Dragon

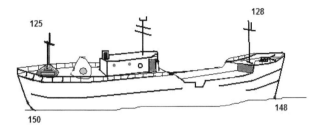

Notes: This wreck is not very well known by the general diving community, but does have a very interesting history of smuggling human cargo. It also sank fairly recently, so is still in pretty good condition, and is deep enough to escape most of the significant storm damage that tears up some of the shallower wrecks. The location can be found on NOAA chart #18433 as a standard wreck symbol.

The *Black Dragon* is also in an out-of-the-way location for U.S. based divers. However, several charters do run out to this wreck throughout the year from Victoria, Anacortes, and the San Juan Islands. A list of dive charters for technical and some of the more delicate wrecks can be found on our web site at northwestwreckdives.com.

Cautions: Heavy currents on a deep wreck with loose cables can complicate diving this site. At this depth it is all too easy to accumulate significant decompression which must be completed in what are, at times, difficult environmental conditions. There also seems to be a lot of cave line running willy-nilly around the *Black Dragon*, so watch for entanglement hazards. Our advice would be to dive this wreck using a charter on your first go-round.

Name:	**Bloody Mary**
Location:	Lake Washington, Rainier Beach
Position:	**47° 31.3237' N 122° 15.1098' W**
Depth:	**105-115'**
Access:	**Boat Dive**, ramps at Atlantic City ½ mile west or Gene Coulon Park 2.5 miles southeast.
Rating:	**Advanced,** due to depth and low visibility.
Currents:	**None.**

History: The *Bloody Mary* is another little boat with an anonymous past. Our guess is that she was a small utility launch used for towing or light cargo work. The vessel's small size and the proximity of the exhaust pipe, which runs right up the center of the pilot house, make it unlikely that she was used in any passenger capacity. The wooden hull and carved deck cleats date her sinking to be at least 60 years ago.

Dive Information: A silt bank on the south side near the keel rises to the height of the pilot house. It is easy to stir up a veil of billowing mud if you are facing north. One spin around the wreck should only take a few minutes. There are quite a few nice features to see in each section of the boat.

Notes: This is an enjoyable little wreck. However, she is small, so only two or three divers can crowd around her at any one time. Buoyancy control is vital here or no one is going to see much of anything.

Cautions: This will be a dark, silty, and challenging dive unless you are extremely careful. Running a spool to the wreck from your up-line is a good idea and attention to your bottom time and gas supply is important.

Bloody Mary

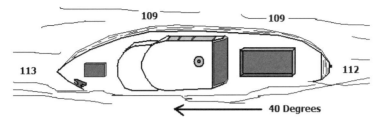

Name: **Boot (double-ender)**

Location: Lake Washington, Rainier Beach

Position: **47° 31.3573' N   122° 15.2515' W**

Depth: **110-120'**

Access: **Boat Dive**, ramps at Atlantic City 1/3 mile west or Gene Coulon Park 2.5 miles southeast.

Rating: **Advanced,** due to depth and low visibility.

History: The *Boot* is a double-ended utility launch with a steel-riveted hull. She is clearly from a bygone era, and most likely was used to transport small groups of people back and forth on the lake before being scuttled.

Dive Information: This 27-foot boat has a very interesting steering apparatus near the bow. The steering wheel stands quite tall and must have been operated while standing.   The hull now sits on a silt mound at a depth of about 120 feet.

Notes/Cautions: This is a fun little wreck. It isn't the best out there, but it is worth a short dive if you are in the south end of the lake. The *Boot* is deep and dark enough to get you into trouble, so use caution and common sense.

Name:	**Boss**
Location:	Blakely Harbor, South Bainbridge Island
Position:	**47° 35.4652' N 122° 29.7665' W**
Depth:	**50'**
Access:	**Boat Dive**, Don Armeni Boat ramp is located 5 miles east or Manchester ramp 4 miles south.
Rating:	**Beginner.**
Currents:	**Negligible** in all but extreme tidal exchanges.

History: Sitting on a shallow, muddy bottom in Blakely Harbor is a pair of wrecks, infamous locally as *The Boss*. Little is known about the origin of these wrecks, other than they were most likely scuttled at this "out of the way" location. The *Boss* itself is about 70 feet long and was most likely a fishing boat. Today, her wood hull is lying with a slight port list in fifty feet of water. The bow of the vessel points towards Seattle, which is only six miles away. Much of the wreck stands proud of the bottom, including a large bow nearly ten feet high.

The middle of the wreck has collapsed where the *Employee* was purposely sunk on top of the *Boss*. This 30-foot utility vessel is a recent addition. The engine, gauges, and many artifacts are still in place. The *Employee* is pointed east and is sitting with its stern right on top of the starboard bulwarks of the larger boat. The decks are only 35-40 feet deep. Historically, this is very popular with local dive charter operators. They will often attach a buoy to the wreck which makes this an easy site to find and dive.

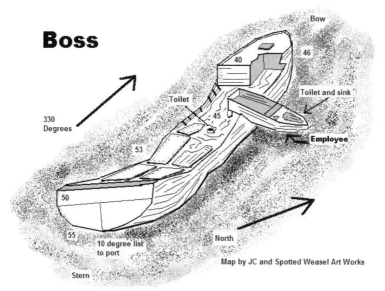

Boss

Bow

46

40

Toilet and sink

Toilet

45

330
Degrees

Employee

53

North

50

55

10 degree list
to port

Map by JC and Spotted Weasel Art Works

Stern

Dive Information: The bow of the *Boss* is intact and you can look inside where the fishermen once ate, slept and complained about the captain. There are small relics of the wheelhouse littering the forward section and thousands of brass screws holding the planks together. Heading aft, the midship is broken down and you will pass the stern of the *Employee* on the starboard rail. The stern of the *Boss* is amazingly well preserved, with a steering lazarette that is open all the way down to the keel. Much of the construction details of this boat are open and waiting for an inspection by curious divers.

Notes: The mud bottom offers good anchorage. The boats are very easy to pick up on a fish finder, with 10-15 feet of vertical rise from the bottom to the top of the wrecks. This site makes an excellent second dive to many of the sites in and around Blakely Harbor. We typically launch at Manchester when visiting this wreck, but the Alki boat ramp is only 5 miles due east as well.

Cautions: This is a very easy wreck to dive and is well protected from our typical southerly winds. However, it can get a bit bouncy when the wind blows out of the north or when the Winslow Ferry goes by.

Name:	**Bruce Higgins Underwater Trails**
Location:	Edmonds, Puget Sound
Position:	**47° 48.8353' N 122° 23.1188' W**
Depth:	**30'**
Access:	**Shore Dive**, City of Edmonds Park.
Rating:	**Beginner.**
Currents:	**Edmonds**, WSW of Port Madison.

History: Edmonds Underwater Park is probably the most popular dive location in the Pacific Northwest. It is shallow (35 feet) with very easy shore access provided via a park well maintained by the City of Edmonds. The site has restrooms and changing rooms as well as a fresh water shower for rinsing off divers and their gear. Volunteer divers, led by Bruce Higgins, have placed an amazing assortment of diver enhancements and wrecks in the underwater portion of the park, making this dive site worthy of several visits.

Dive Information: There are numerous wrecks that have been sunk in the park over the years. They began with the sinking of the *Alitak* on top of the wreck of the *De Lion Dry Dock* in 1972 and continue at regular intervals. For the explorer in all of us, the Bruce Higgins Underwater Trails is a great place to learn about wreck diving. You can observe firsthand a wide variety of vessels in various states of deterioration as Mother Nature reclaims them. For the critter watcher, the old wrecks are now artificial reefs which are loaded with life. You'll find colorful nudibranchs and schools of juvenile rockfish as well as massive ling cod and cabezon that are not afraid of divers.

Here is a partial list of the wrecks found in the park:

De Lion Dry Dock, a 325-foot long structure, sunk in 1935 as protection for the ferry terminal;

Alitak, a 94-foot long wood hulled tug sunk on top of the very east end of the dry dock in 1972;

Fossil, sunk to the northwest of the dry dock in 1982;

Molly Brown, sunk in 1996;

Triumph, 70-foot long wood tug sunk in 1999. Marked by a white buoy with a dive flag. Very popular with divers;

H.R. Jackson, located along jetty way, straight out from the jetty;

Cinclant, located along jetty way, very close to the jetty;

Genius, located southeast of the *Triumph*;

Cupid, located due east of the *Triumph*;

Mesmerized, located due east of the *Triumph*;

Glacey, located near the end of Centennial Way;

Seabus, located next to the *Glacey*;

Melinda II, located at the intersection of Cathedral and Telegraph way.

Notes: There is a large map showing all of the park's amazing underwater features that is posted on the wall of the restrooms/changing rooms. It is kept up to date and should be your first stop when planning your dives in the park.

Cautions: The *De Lion Dry Dock* and *Alitak* are located right next to a working ferry. Be very careful not to surface in the way of or under the ferry. It is best to dive these features when the current is running to the north.

Name:	**Burton**
Location:	Gig Harbor
Position:	**47° 19.8670' N 122° 34.6781' W**
Depth:	**40-45'**
Access:	**Boat Dive**, ramps in Gig Harbor ½ mile northwest or at Point Defiance 3.4 miles east.
Rating:	**Intermediate** due to boat traffic.
Currents:	**Negligible.**

History: The steamship *Burton* lies forgotten on the bottom of Gig Harbor just west of the popular Tides Tavern dock. This 93-foot long wooden steamer was built in 1905 and served as a passenger and cargo ferry in the early 1900's. After 23 years of faithful service in the Mosquito Fleet, she was retired and tied up to the People's Wharf that now services the Tides Tavern.

On the night of February 22, 1924, she was consumed by fire and was towed out to the center of the harbor so as not to endanger the other boats. There she sank and still sits today as a fascinating journey into our local maritime history.

The *Burton* is infamous for developing one of the biggest feuds in the history of the Mosquito Fleet. She was paired off against the steamer *Vashon*, with the two bitter rivals making three runs a day between Tacoma and Vashon Island. They would leave the dock at the same time and would race to see who could pick up the waiting passengers first. Side by side, nearly touching (and sometimes bumping), they would steam full speed while hurling curses and insults at each other. This often terrified passengers and more than once resulted in fist fights between the crewmembers of the adversarial boats.

Burton

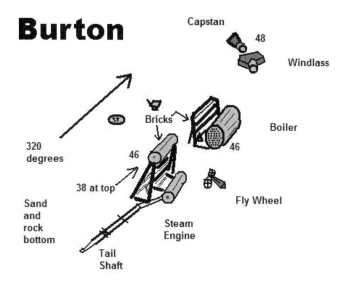

Capstan

48

Windlass

Bricks

Boiler

320 degrees

46

46

38 at top

Sand and rock bottom

Fly Wheel

Steam Engine

Tail Shaft

Dive Information: Diving the *S.S. Burton* is very easy and shallow. It is only 40 feet deep in a very protected harbor. The sandy bottom offers good anchorage with very little current. Unfortunately, the wreck lies right in the main navigation channel, just off the end of the dock at the Gig Harbor Marina.

Notes: The boiler and steam engine are easy to locate on a fish finder and each of the boiler tubes now harbors grunt sculpins, decorated warbonnets, or baby octopus. This is a great site for macro photography. There isn't much of the 97 ton wood hull left, but scattered about are pieces of deck machinery and piping, as well as the fire bricks that surrounded the boiler. These are covered with prolific marine life which makes for a very interesting dive.

Cautions: This harbor is a very busy. It is really only safe to dive this wreck in the winter when boat traffic is at a minimum. Be sure to keep someone in the boat and to fly a dive flag to alert the captains passing by that there are divers in the water.

Name:	Cabezon
Location:	Anacortes, southwest of Guemes Island
Position:	48° 31.8112' N 122° 40.2192' W
Depth:	60-70'
Access:	**Boat Dive**, ramps at Washington Park 2 miles southeast or Anacortes 5 miles east.
Rating:	**Advanced** due to high currents.
Currents:	**Bellingham Channel.**

History: Little is known of the history of the fishing vessel that we call the *Cabezon*. The twin-screwed vessel is about 100 feet long and obviously caught fire before being towed out into the channel southwest of Guemes Island to sink. The location of the vessel is well marked on NOAA charts. It is just 750 yards due south of the red number four bell buoy which marks the south entrance to Bellingham Channel between Guemes and Cypress Islands.

Dive Information: Diving the *Cabezon* can be challenging due to the high currents coming in or out of Bellingham Channel. Plan your dive on a day with a small exchange and run a live boat to pick up any divers that are swept away by the moving water. The wreck is only about 60 feet deep and contains a lot of machinery to look at. It also harbors some of the largest ling cod and cabezon that I have ever seen. This is where the wreck snagged the name "*Cabezon*."

Notes: The twin engines of the *Cabezon* are still in place along with the propellers and much of the deck gear used on this hard-working fishing boat. Several large sheaves that once hauled the fishing gear on deck are also scattered throughout the wreckage.

Cabezon

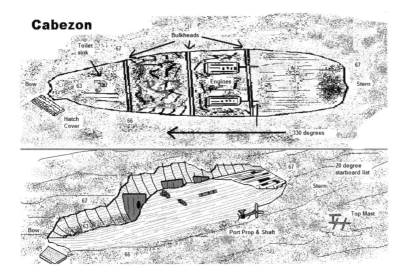

The top of the mast is located to the south of the wreck with a large air horn still attached. This is an interesting find out in the middle of a relatively barren expanse of mud. We often dive this site on our way back to Anacortes from the San Juan Islands. It makes a nice treat for the wreck divers on the boat after days of "critter dives" around the islands.

Cautions: Boat traffic can be heavy heading into and out of Anacortes so be very careful not to dive this site during ebbing tides where it would be easy to get swept into the shipping lanes. Keep an experienced skipper on the boat with a sharp lookout for the divers and other boats in the area.

When surfacing away from the shot line, it is always a good idea to deploy a large surface marker buoy to alert your boat and other boats in the area of the diver's location. You can drift quite a ways away from this wreck while hanging for a three minute safety stop.

Name:	**Carkeek Park Wreck**
Location:	Carkeek Park, North Seattle
Position:	**47° 42.6553' N 122° 23.1916' W**
Depth:	**70-80'**
Access:	**Boat Dive**, ramps at Shilshole 1.5 miles south or Port Townsend . Possible shore dive but a very long swim.
Rating:	**Intermediate, due to depth.**
Currents:	**West Point.**

History: We found this boat while searching for the *Dauntless*. The wreck is of recent construction, judging from the numerous PVC parts that are present. It was likely abandoned and sank due to neglect prior to 1995.

Dive Information: The bottom at this site is flat and sandy. The visibility here is usually decent and stays good even when people churn it up. The wreck itself is small but has enough interesting features to keep you occupied for a short time. It is not a difficult dive for those familiar with this area, but is just slightly deeper than what is recommended for a novice diver.

As with most of the dives in our area, you can expect some current. It is important to watch the conditions and to plan your dive so it is not right in the middle of a very large tidal exchange.

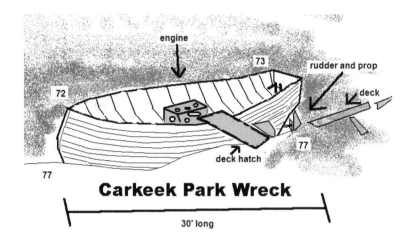

engine

73

rudder and prop

deck

72

deck hatch

77

77

Carkeek Park Wreck

30' long

Notes: This is a good dive followed by the *Dauntless* (which is a better, shallower dive).   It is a fun little wreck to bounce around with the engine exposed and the hull still complete. It would also be an interesting navigational challenge to try to locate this wreck from shore. If you can hit this target while following a compass bearing from the beach, you are a very good navigator!

The wreck is located nearly 330 yards offshore on a bearing of 240° magnetic from the Piper Creek trestle (where the creek runs under the railroad) on Carkeek Park Beach.

Cautions: If you are attempting this from shore, it is directly off of the park, but it is a long, long swim out and back.   The dive is much more pleasant from a boat or could be a fun scooter dive from the park.

Name:	Comet
Location:	Port Hadlock, Port Townsend Bay.
Position:	**48° 01.9852' N 122° 45.0570' W**
Depth:	**15-40'**
Access:	**Shore Dive**, from the Port Hadlock boat ramp.
Rating:	**Beginner.**
Currents:	**Negligible.**

History: The *Comet,* a 127-foot ocean-going tug, was built in Long Beach, California, in 1944 (*LT 393*) to haul barges across the Pacific for the war effort. By the time the boat was completed, the war was over. A fishing company bought the tug and, for many years, she worked in Alaska. After a fire, the vessel was hauled to Lake Washington and refurbished as a "cruise boat" to take tourists around the lake. It caught fire again in 1966 and sank. The wood hull was then re-floated, and the engines and machinery were salvaged.

Emily and Fred (no last name) bought the almost-empty boat in 1975 for $500.00 and had it moved to Poulsbo. They lived communally in a big house on the beach with a group of "free spirited" individuals. Three or four others lived on the boat. They had built bunks in the forecastle and installed a wood stove. The plan was to re-fit the *Comet* and turn it into a three-masted sailboat and cruise to Costa Rica. However, the commune broke up after 1976 and the neglected *Comet* was towed to Port Hadlock where she eventually sank.

Dive Information: This wreck is an easy to access shore dive just off of the Port Hadlock boat ramp at the south end of Port Townsend Bay. The vessel is lying on its starboard side 200 feet south of the boat ramp.

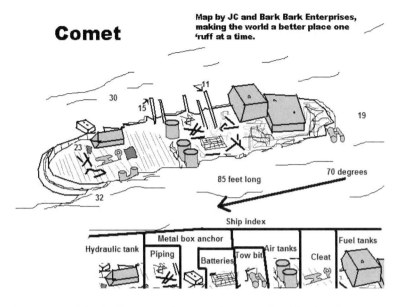

Comet

Map by JC and Bark Bark Enterprises, making the world a better place one 'ruff at a time.

30
11
15
19
23
70 degrees
85 feet long
32

Ship index

Hydraulic tank
Metal box anchor
Piping
Batteries
Tow bit
Air tanks
Cleat
Fuel tanks

To access this shallow wreck from shore, park at the boat ramp and gear up. Then walk (or swim) less than 200 feet south along the shore until you come to the "Clam Farm, Keep Out" sign on the beach. Enter the water and swim down the slope. You'll find the bow of the *Comet* in only 15 feet of water (visible at low tides).

As you continue to swim astern (east) on the wreck, you'll see a slim wood hull slowly deteriorating under the onslaught of the salt water and boring worms. The aft end of the wreck sits in about 40 feet of water. Several large fuel and hydraulic tanks are sitting in the remains of the engine room.

Notes: The location of this wreck is well-marked on NOAA chart #18464 as a boat-shaped obstruction.

Cautions: Be aware of the possibility of boat traffic from the nearby Port Hadlock Boat Ramp and any fishermen on shore that might be casting their lures your way.

Name:	**Concrete Sailboat**
Location:	Budd Inlet, Olympia
Position:	**47° 05.2357' N 122° 55.8407' W**
Depth:	**40'**
Access:	**Boat Dive**, ramps at Swantown 2.2 miles south southeast and Boston Harbor 3.3 miles north northeast.
Rating:	**Intermediate,** due to low visibility and entanglement hazards.
Currents:	**Weak and variable.**

History: We were unable to locate the true tale about this wrecked 45-foot concrete-hulled sailboat. It appears to have sunk while someone was working on a Frankenstein-like project. There are a large number of blue plastic barrels floating underwater that are attached to the wreck. The wreck is well marked on NOAA chart #18445 with a classic wreck symbol and the word "Masts."

Dive Information: There is not much tidal exchange in Budd Inlet, so visibility at this site is typically pretty poor. The wreck itself sits upright on the bottom in about 40 feet of water. There you will find the tangled wreckage with masts, booms, cables and semi-floating barrels lying around, which can be confusing.

However, if you swim around the deck a few times and compare the wreckage to Jeff's excellent map, the layout will "gel" in your mind. Then you'll find orienting yourself a bit easier. There is a large orange buoy permanently attached to the wreck to warn boaters away, which makes locating and diving this site pretty darn easy.

Concrete Sailboat

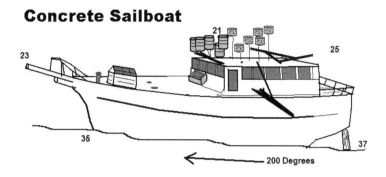

Notes: The first time you dive here, it tends to be a bit spooky due to the low visibility and the cluttered wreckage, even for very experienced divers. The wreck has three levels, so there is plenty to explore once you get in the water.

The wood rudder is in place at the stern. An odd looking doghouse is built into the bow (wow) deck. There are all kinds of interesting items to see if you poke your head through the doors into the various levels of the wreck. However, I wouldn't go inside. This vessel has been down there a long time and most of the wood is rotten and may crumble if disturbed.

Your exhaust bubbles could easily cause the roof of the cabin to collapse. Penetration is probably not a good idea on this old sailboat.

Cautions: Low visibility, boat traffic, a multitude of entanglement hazards and lots of overly friendly jellyfish in the summer make this one of those dives that is not for everyone. However, if you happen to be in south Puget Sound and are looking for something different, this concrete monstrosity will certainly pique your interest.

Name:	**Cynthia Sea**
Location:	Hood Canal Bridge, Termination Point
Position:	**47° 51.917' N 122° 38.105' W**
Depth:	**70'**
Access:	**Boat Dive**, ramp on the west end of the Hood Canal Bridge.
Rating:	**Advanced,** due to high currents.
Currents:	**Port Gamble Bay entrance.**

History: The vessel name is unknown, so we refer to it as the *Cynthia Sea*. The story behind this wrecked 30-foot sailboat has been lost. It looks as though the boat collided with the bridge, as the bow has significant damage. Evidence suggests that this fiberglass sailboat has been a wreck for quite a few years.

Dive Information: The *Cynthia Sea* rests upright at the south end of the main Hood Canal Bridge wreckage, just south of the floating portion of the new bridge. A broken mast and sail lie amidships. A mere fifteen feet to the north lies the roadbed of the sunken bridge, which offers one of the most spectacular dives in the region.

The remains of the old bridge is carpeted with anemones, sponges and a multitude of wildlife that will glow in the beam of a good dive light. The wreck of the sailboat sits on the southern edge of the (formerly) floating section of the bridge. The *Cynthia Sea* can be hard to distinguish from the rest of the wreckage simply because of the scale and tangled nature of the bridge.

Hood Canal Bridge, West Side

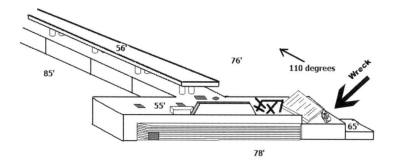

Notes: This is a very serious dive and should not be attempted without extensive current and navigation experience. Plan this dive around slack water on a very small tidal exchange and be willing to thumb the dive if conditions don't look right. Remember, they are called current "predictions" for a reason.

Diving directly under the Hood Canal Bridge is forbidden, so straying even a few feet north of the wreck on scuba is not allowed. There are big signs posted under the new bridge that caution "No Diving," so don't say we didn't warn you.

Cautions: Boat traffic is frequent and can present a significant danger. Currents can get ripping here very quickly as all of Hood Canal's tidal exchange is flowing through this rather narrow portion. Do not attempt to dive this wreck if you are not comfortable and well experienced in extreme current and difficult navigation conditions.

For those of you who are up for the challenge, it is truly spectacular. It really is too bad that the bridge itself isn't open for divers to enjoy.

Name:	**Dauntless**
Location:	Seattle, Puget Sound
Position:	**47° 42.1315' N 122° 23.9984' W**
Depth:	**55'**
Access:	**Boat Dive**, ramp at Shilshole 1 mile south.
Rating:	**Beginner.**
Currents:	**West Point.**

History: The remains of the Mosquito Fleet Steamer *Dauntless* rest forgotten off of Meadow Point just north of Golden Garden Park in Seattle. They have been there since December 30, 1923, when a fierce storm blew the well known steamer loose from her moorings at Kingston. She drifted across the Sound and piled up on the beach near Meadow Point, a total loss.

For visitors, the wreck of the *Dauntless* is a pleasant dive back into a time when the Mosquito Fleet of steamers were the primary mode of transportation in and around Puget Sound. The *Dauntless* was typical of those Steamers at 93 feet long and 91 tons. The wood burning vessel was built near Tacoma in 1899 and she ran the Seattle - Tacoma (East Pass) route for many years after the turn of the century. She was eventually replaced by the much faster *Defiance*. She then skipped around the sound until settling into the route between Seattle and Port Ludlow for many years prior to her stormy demise.

Historic and current underwater photos of the steamship *Dauntless* can be viewed by visiting our web site at northwestwreckdives.com.

Dauntless

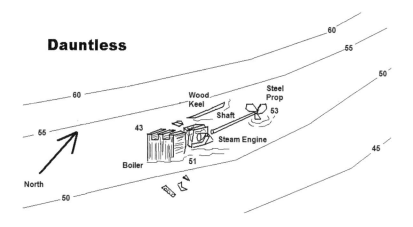

Dive Information: The six-foot-diameter steel propeller sits attached to the tail shaft, which runs all the way to the remains of a large gearbox and triple expansion engine. Most, but not all, of the old wood hull has rotted away. Bits and pieces of machinery still provide habitat for many rockfish, ling cod, and kelp greenlings that peer out at divers and wonder what all the fuss is about.

Notes: Large piles of fire brick surround the remains of the old boiler which once pushed the "too slow" *Dauntless* up and down Puget Sound in the heyday of the old steamers of the Mosquito Fleet. Visiting the old girl is like traveling back into a very interesting period of local history and well worth the trip out to this dive site for you history buffs. The *Carkeek Park Wreck* is located just north of the *Dauntless*, offering a nearby alternate or second dive.

Cautions: This site does get some current, so diving near slack would be prudent. Also, watch out for fishing nets, crab traps, and boat traffic from nearby Shilshole Marina.

Name:	**Des Moines Wreck**
Location:	Normandy Park, Puget Sound
Position:	**47° 24.657' N 122° 20.584' W**
Depth:	**40-55'**
Access:	**Boat Dive**, ramps at Redondo 4 miles south or Des Moines lift 1 mile east.
Rating:	**Beginner.**
Currents:	**Blake Island, negligible**.

History: This once beautiful wood-hulled yacht caught fire and sank just outside of the Des Moines Marina in 1994. The hull is a bright blue but has collapsed along the starboard side due in part to poor anchoring techniques. She is approximately 55 feet in length. Many recognizable bits and pieces of the old boat are scattered throughout the wreckage. A large fuel tank sits above the twin rudders, but the propellers have been removed.

This wreck has been a popular dive site and is frequently visited by local charters operating out of Central Puget Sound. The popularity of and easy access to this site make this a great experience for the beginning wreck or boat diver. She is easy to locate for first time boat skippers and the mild currents allow diving in all but the very worst conditions.

Please use care when anchoring on this or any wreck site. We have observed that a number of our local wrecks have suffered heavy damage from large anchors being dropped directly onto the wreck. It is much better to anchor just to the side of the wreckage, and run a reel allowing returning divers to easily locate the anchor line.

Des Moines Wreck

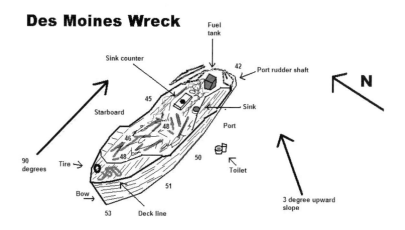

Dive Information: The location of this wreck, just north of the Des Moines Marina, is not very current sensitive. This site makes a good second dive after the KVI Tower (4 miles due west) and is easily found by locating the impressive and large, three tier stairway structure in front of Normandy Beach Park. Head northwest along the 50-foot depth contour and the wreckage is easy to spot on a depth finder at the coordinates listed.

Notes: Photographers and critter divers should also spend a little time exploring the flat, muddy bottom around the wreck. Careful observation will frequently reveal lots of interesting critters hiding in the "muck" near the artificial reef provided by the wreck site.

Cautions: Keep clear of the boat traffic coming in to and out of the Des Moines Marina. Observe the current before diving and watch for crab pots and jellyfish in the area.

Name: **Diamond Girl**

Location: South Lake Washington

Position: **47° 31.4069' N   122° 15.4240' W**

Depth: **100-105'**

Access: **Boat Dive,** ramps at Atlantic City ¼ mile west or Gene Coulon Park 2.5 miles southeast.

Rating: **Advanced,** due to depth, low visibility.

Currents: **Negligible.**

History: The *Diamond Girl* is one of many wrecks scuttled in the south end of Lake Washington. The name comes from the impressive diamond plate that decorates the wreck and covers the forward section of this 35-foot motorsailer.

Dive Information: The *Diamond Girl* sank in more than 100 feet of low visibility water. There is little light penetration, which makes this a very dark wreck. One of her sails is hanging out of the bow hatch, but there is no mast (probably removed before it was scuttled) and not much in the way of interesting deck gear.

Notes: If you are making a day at the south end of the lake, it is another one to hit but it is not worth a special trip out just to dive the "*D-Girl.*" The dive map for this wreck is located in the appendices at the back of the book.

Cautions: Depth, darkness in the lake, and silt around the wreck make this a dive that should be taken a bit more seriously. Take at least two lights, stay off the bottom, and watch your bottom time.

Name:	**Diamond Knot**
Location:	Crescent Bay, Strait of Juan de Fuca
Position:	**48°10.300' N 123° 42.614' W**
Depth:	**70-140'**
Access:	**Boat Dive**, ramp for large boats at Port Angeles 12 miles east, small boats can launch at Fresh Water Bay at high tide 3.5 miles east.
Rating:	**Advanced**, due to depth and currents.
Currents:	**Angeles Point, strong currents.**

History: The *Diamond Knot* was built during WWII as a coastal motorship. She sank on August 13, 1947 in a foggy collision with the steamer *Fen Victory* just South of Race Rocks near Victoria, Canada. Two Foss tugs attempted to bring the stricken vessel into the shallow waters of Crescent Bay. The strong currents and the water flowing in through the gashed hull caused the freighter to sink to her watery grave in the early morning hours.

The 154,000 cases of canned Alaska salmon she carried was worth $3.5 million in 1947! A unique salvage effort ensued where 70 percent of the cargo was recovered, and the middle of the ship still shows signs of the salvage operation.

Dive Information: The *Diamond Knot* is often considered the pinnacle of our recreational dive sites.   The steel-hulled wreck is 338 feet long and is about 50 feet wide. Current is nearly always a factor and can be severe, changing rapidly in direction and ferocity during the course of even a short dive.

The stern, which still has the massive superstructure in place, is lying on its starboard side. The bridge looks forward over the remaining wreckage and two large masts are attached. Numerous walkways and deck machines are present as you swim back to the elegantly rounded stern. The port side of the hull rises up to around 70 feet of depth.

Amidships is a jumble of steel plates and two gigantic crane derricks (kingposts). They rise some 40 feet above the deck and the booms are visible in the wreckage below. The salvagers left this section in disarray, and a significant portion of the hull was cut away to access the canned salmon in the holds.

The bow is resting at a 45-degree angle to starboard (south) and is the smallest segment of this mighty ship, about 60 feet long. The anchors are in place in their hawse holes and the large chain is tight on the windlasses. On the bow, divers can do the "Titanic" at around 90 feet of depth, with the sand 25 feet below. Of course you'll have to bring your own Kate Winslet on this dive.

Diamond Knot

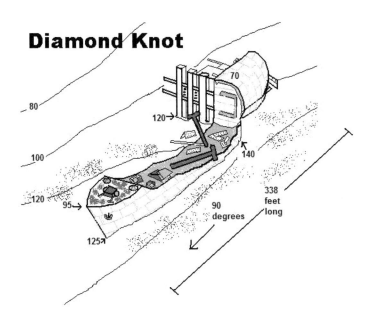

Notes: The best way to dive the *Diamond Knot* is to go with someone who has been there before. There are seasonal charters and local divers that go out to the wreck. Experience is required to dive this site safely.

Cautions: Current planning, a willingness to wait until the dive looks safe, navigation along a large and confusing wreck, safe ascents, signaling the boat while below that you are ascending off the anchor, and knowing when it is simply not safe to dive this wreck are imperative skills here. The payoff is an awesome dive on one of the "best of the best" wrecks in the Northwest. However, be advised that this wreck has teeth and can bite. Finally, a light-hearted diver tradition has emerged over the years involving the name. If you have done a dive on it, you may refer to it as "The Knot," otherwise you should use her full name.

Name:	The Dockton Five

Location: Dockton Harbor, Maury Island

Positions:
47° 22.4057' N 122° 27.3853' W Tricabin
47° 22.5041' N 122° 27.4193' W Cruiser
47° 22.4976' N 122° 27.5017' W Sailboat
47° 22.5013' N 122° 27.5686' W Sailboat
47° 22.4873' N 122° 27.5713' W Meatloaf

Depth: 30-45'

Access: **Shore or Boat Dive**, enter at the Dockton boat ramp 750 feet southeast or launch at the Point Defiance boat ramp 5 miles south.

Rating: Beginner.

Currents: Negligible.

History: The stories of the demise of these wrecks is buried in a forgotten past. More than likely they all sank while moored in the harbor due to general neglect.

Dive Information: The *Tricabin* is in 35 feet of water and is about 32 feet long. The *Cruiser* is around 40 feet long and is in 40 feet of water (that one is easy to remember). The other three are all about 20 feet long and in 33-37 feet of water. Visibility in the harbor is sometimes good; sometimes it is not so good (as in you can't see your own fins unless you are less than 4 feet tall).

The wrecks of the *Cruiser* and *Tricabin* are the best of the bunch and make for an interesting afternoon of diving. They stand upright and are in good condition with radios and radar in place, windows intact and the paint bright on the hulls. Peer through the sliding glass doors of the *Cruiser* and it is obvious that this wreck has not been on the bottom all that long.

Cruiser

The sailboats are smaller, but are fun to take a swim around. The *Meatloaf* is tired and in pretty bad shape, much like the singer it was named after.

Notes: This is a great place to work on navigating from one target to another underwater whether you are shore diving or boat diving. The wrecks are in close enough proximity to do several on one tank of air.

If your navigation and/or anchoring skills are not up to the task, you can enjoy a nice dive hopelessly searching in the mud for a wreck you think is there, but might be just ten feet away. Not that we've had any experiences like that, but a search and discovery dive is always an option.

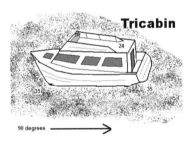

Tricabin

A reel that is tied to your anchor line will help you find your way back to that line in order to ascend safely near your boat.

Cautions: These wrecks are located in a working harbor which isn't very busy. However, there are boats occasionally going in and out. Carry a surface marker buoy with you and deploy it before you ascend if you can't find your way back to the anchor line. This helps nearby boaters to avoid running over you (and helps provide entertainment for jetskis in the area).

Name:	**Dungeness Crane**
Location:	Dungeness Spit, Strait of Juan de Fuca
Position:	**48° 10.482' N 123° 10.556' W**
Depth:	**60-90'**
Access:	**Boat Dive**, ramps at Port Angeles 11.6 miles west or at Sequim 10 miles southeast.
Rating:	**Advanced.**
Currents:	**Angeles Point, very strong currents.**

History: Little is known about the origin of one of the most magnificent wreck dives in the Strait of Juan de Fuca. A large *Manitowac* pedestal crane rests on the bottom of the current swept strait providing refuge for an amazing multitude of marine creatures. The members of the 130 foot boom and "A" frame are completely covered with brilliant sponges (and the nudibranchs that eat them).

The base of the crane, which once was attached to a pedestal on a crane barge or self-loading log barge, dwarfs divers that swim by. The fast line jib and sheaves remain in place as if waiting to pick up their next load of cargo. The control cabin is so overgrown with sponges and giant barnacles that very few divers will recognize its function, but it is still there, along with the boom pendants and blocks.

Dive Information: This wreck is marked on NOAA charts and the boom structure makes it a fairly easy wreck to "drag and snag" (see anchoring techniques). The top of the crane house is only sixty feet deep. There is an incredible amount of marine life using the wreck as an artificial reef. Numerous wolf eels peer out from the engine room and hide among the hoist spools in the crane house.

Dungeness Spit Crane

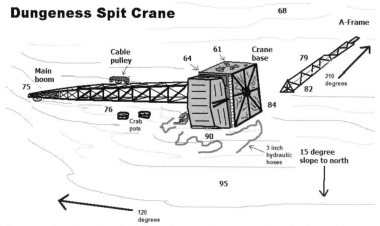

Large schools of rockfish and greenlings can also be found hiding from the currents, so take the time to have a leisurely swim along the full length of the crane boom. Also, spend some time peering into all of the nooks and crannies of the crane house.

Notes: Diving this wreck requires a common sense approach to the heavy currents that sweep through this area. Even on minimal exchanges that show predicted currents of zero, we've been blown off this wreck more than once. When you arrive at the site and anchor, wait until the current calms down before entering the water. That will ensure you have an absolutely gorgeous dive on a site that is not only covered with marine life, but is one of my all time favorites. Having the first diver tie the anchor into the wreck is prudent at this site, as is having a qualified driver remain in the boat to pick up any divers that are forced off the wreck by currents.

Cautions: Plan your dives carefully so you don't exceed your allowed bottom time, carry a large surface marker buoy deployable from depth, and keep your eye on the current. Flapping in the howling current like a flag in a gale on your safety stop is just not a lot of fun!

Dungeness Spit Crane Boom

Name:	**Easy Eight**
Location:	Dungeness Spit, Strait of Juan de Fuca
Position:	**48° 10.0033' N 123° 12.1933' W**
Depth:	**60-65'**
Access:	**Boat Dive**, ramps at Port Angeles 10 miles west or at Sequim 11 miles southeast.
Rating:	**Advanced.**
Currents:	**Angeles Point, very strong currents.**

History: The thirty-four foot fishing vessel *Easy Eight* sank during a storm on November 13, 1992.

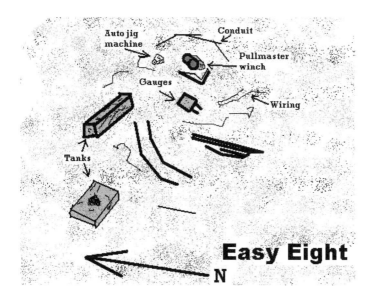

Dive Information: There is not much of this small wood-hulled commercial fishing vessel left. Evidence of her fishing career are a small Pullmaster winch and a commercial jigging machine.

The wreckage is scattered over an area about 60 feet by 50 feet. Tanks, gauges and other debris are strewn around with very little wood remaining from the hull or keel.

Notes: This wreck is near the *Dungeness Crane* and *Martha Foss* tug and may be worth a visit after you have fully explored the other two. The challenge of this wreck can be in simply finding it. The position is correct but there is very little relief off the bottom to identify it.

Cautions: The current at all of the wrecks in the Strait can be extremely strong. There are no rocks or parts of the wreck for divers to hide behind. Keep a boat tender watching down current and be prepared to get out of there when it picks up.

Name: **El Captain**

Location: Friday Harbor, San Juan Island

Position: **48° 32.5543' N   123° 00.9797' W**

Depth: **10-33'**

Access: **Boat Dive,** Friday Harbor.

Rating: **Beginner.**

Currents: **Negligible.**

History: A fifty foot, wood-hulled, ex-U.S. Navy motor launch that had been converted to a commercial dive boat and renamed *El Captain* sank due to a fire in March 1995.

Dive Information: Resting on the bottom like it was being run up on the beach in its last minutes, the bow of the old launch faces the shore of this small bay. You will find very little current in the harbor. Nearly all of the equipment on this boat is gone and evidence suggests that as it burned the fire consumed most of the boat. If you move the kelp that covers this wreck, you'll find the steering gear, gudgeons, and some of the engine room equipment. A unique looking cleat with a capstan on the side lies on the bottom near the starboard bow.

Notes: With a depth that does not exceed 35 feet on an average tide, this is an easy second dive after either the *Two Pump Chump* or *Friday Harbor Barge*.

Cautions: There is quite a bit of boat traffic in Friday Harbor including regular ferry runs. Watch for boats, fly a dive flag, and have a great time.

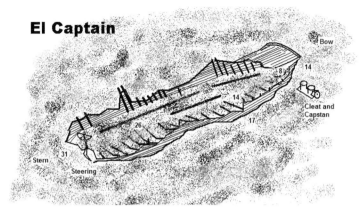

El Captain

Bow

14

8

14

Cleat and
Capstan

26

17

31

Stern

Steering

Bonus Dive

Name: **Friday Harbor Barge**

Location: Friday Harbor, San Juan Island

Position: **48° 31.739' N   123° 00.070' W**

Depth: **25-35'**

Access: **Boat Dive,** Friday Harbor.

Rating: **Beginner.**

History: The *Friday Harbor Barge* was a decked, well built utility barge probably used for landing cargo in remote places in the San Juan Islands in years gone by.

Dive Notes: This is a large barge with many holes and places for things to hide. It is in a very low current area, so there is little life here compared with other sites in the San Juans, but it is possible to dive this just about anytime. Any port in a storm?

77

Name:	**Ferndale**
Location:	Jones Bay, Lopez Island
Position:	**48° 26.7221' N 122° 53.4337' W**
Depth:	**20-30'**
Access:	**Boat Dive**, ramps at Anacortes 12 miles northeast or Sequim 20 miles southwest.
Rating:	**Beginner.**
Currents:	**Negligible.**

History: The 110-foot long, 150 ton steamship *Ferndale*, was hauling a load of china and lime from the old lime kiln on San Juan Island to Port Townsend in December of 1890 when the weather came up. She had been brought up from San Francisco for the island trade, but her career in the waters of Puget Sound was very brief. Large waves blowing out of the Straits forced the *Ferndale* to turn back. The heavy swell broke the guy wires to the smoke stack which then tore off and went adrift. The once proud steamer caught fire and foundered on the rocks in Mackaye Harbor. All twenty-one persons on board narrowly escaped death but were saved and the burning vessel was abandoned and left to sink where she lies today. Her cargo of five hundred barrels of lime has long since washed away.

Dive Information: The *Ferndale's* boiler is an immense object that is completely covered with Turkish Towel kelp. Unobservant divers will swim right by it thinking that the boiler is a big rock. Lift aside the kelp fronds and you'll be rewarded with a virtual critter condominium. Every one of the boiler tubes is now home for some cute creature including grunt sculpins, gunnels, shrimp and crabs. Clouds of krill engulf the boiler, steam engine, reduction gear and other propulsion machinery.

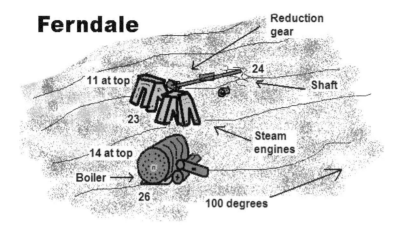

Ferndale

Notes: Careful observation of the bottom around the wreck site will also reveal that in several locations what looks at first glance to be a bottom littered with clam shells is, in fact, broken china from the cargo of the *Ferndale*. I don't think there are any whole pieces left after more than a century of pounding by storms in shallow water, but you never know.

Lots of nudibranchs, rockfish, lings, and many different species of invertebrates make their home in the wreckage. The wood hull is long gone, but for wreck divers, the immense boiler, steam engine, winches, and gearing make for a very interesting dive. This site, at the south end of Lopez Island, is pretty well protected and makes a nice dive for those days when the wind is howling and the exposed sites in the San Juan Islands just aren't safe.

Cautions: The wreck is located quite close to a menacing rock wall and is in the vicinity of some large, propeller eating rocks. Careful seamanship is required to safely drop and recover divers from a live boat at this very old wreck.

Name:	**Four Mile Rock Barges**
Location:	Elliott Bay, Seattle
Positions:	47° 38.415' N 122° 25.640' W
	47° 38.409' N 122° 25.611' W
Depth:	**100'**
Access:	**Boat Dive**, Don Armeni Boat Ramp 3.3 miles southeast or Shilshole 2.4 miles north.
Rating:	**Advanced.**
Currents:	**West Point.**

History: Well marked on nautical charts since the early 70's, the *Four Mile Rock Barges* (aka *West Point Barges*) lie near the 100-foot depth line about a quarter mile offshore from Four Mile Rock. Situated below the Magnolia Bluffs in Seattle, this advanced boat dive was recently in the news as a possible source of "burping oil" seeping into Elliott Bay.

The Coast Guard investigated the wrecks and their divers found no sign of seeping oil. Indeed, on our dives to these two large barges it is apparent that these are both bulk carriers which have no storage tanks to even hold any seeping oil. An old report suggests that a barge sank at this location in a collision with the *Astorian* in 1926. However, it is apparent from the condition of the wrecks that these are much more recent. Perhaps the older barge is buried below them.

Dive Information: The barges are roughly parallel to each other about 50 feet apart. Both are nearly 200 feet long, 50 feet wide and perhaps as tall as 20 feet off the bottom. The deepest part of the wreck would be the stern of the western barge which is just over 100 feet deep at the mud line. The shallower of the two barges lies at only 75 feet of depth.

Notes: The large stabilizing fins on the stern of the barges make a great "cavern" swim through. These are fun to carefully cruise in and out of, parting the schools of rockfish while using careful fin techniques to make sure your buddy doesn't swim through a silt-out! This is a pleasant dive right within sight of downtown Seattle.

Cautions: Both barges are draped with layers of abandoned fishing nets that continue killing year after year. Care must be taken as the nets along with some abandoned cave line poses an entanglement hazard for visiting divers. This is a good site for wreck training as well as for those more experienced recreational divers who are comfortable with the 80-100 foot depths. Be aware that there is a lot of commercial shipping and boat traffic in the area, so fly a dive flag and pay attention to the current.

Name:	**Fox Island Ferry**
Location:	Fox Island, Ferry Dock.
Position:	**47° 15.554' N 122° 37.178' W**
Depth:	**55-65'**
Access:	**Boat Dive**, ramps for small boats at Fox Island Bridge 1.6 miles west, Wollochet 1 mile northeast or larger boats at the Narrows Marina 2.5 miles east southeast.
Rating:	**Intermediate,** due to current.
Currents:	**1:45 before slack at Tacoma Narrows North.**

History: The *Fox Island Ferry* once ran passengers and cargo from Fox Island to Titlow Beach. When the Fox Island Bridge was completed in 1954, the ferry was put out of business and was most likely abandoned at the dock. At some point in the past the neglected vessel sank in about sixty feet of water just off the end of the pilings that make up the wing walls of the dock.

Dive Information: The dock itself was once a very popular shore dive, but it has been fenced off and is now only available via boat. The pilings of the dock are covered with anemones and interesting invertebrates. Heading out from the east wing wall to a depth of sixty feet and turning right, divers will discover the remains of this little ferry. It is located nearly straight off of the old docking apparatus. On the bottom, you will find an engine, fuel tank, reduction gear, shaft, and a cutlass bearing. None of the old wood hull remains.

The sandy bottom in this area is featureless with the exception of an old toilet from the ferry lying slightly north of the wreck.

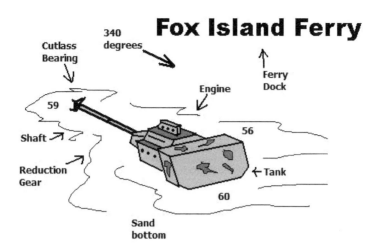

Fox Island Ferry

Cutlass Bearing · 340 degrees · Engine · Ferry Dock · 59 · Shaft · 56 · Reduction Gear · Tank · 60 · Sand bottom

Notes: There is good anchorage on either side of the pilings, and it is a simple matter of swimming out to the depth and doing a short search. Remember, this is not a big wreck so adjust your search depending on tide. At mid-tide looking in 60 feet of water is about right.

The Fox Island Bridge to the west or Z's Reef to the east make an excellent first or second dive along with this old wreck. If you time your dives right, you can also dive the East Wall of Fox Island after you dive this wreck due to the large time difference between slack water at the two sites (about 90 minutes).

Cautions: There can be a lot of boat traffic at this site, especially in the summer! Flying a dive flag may not be enough, so don't surface unless you are under your boat, have a surface marker, or are in the safety of the pilings. There can be quite a bit of current here as well, so plan your dive for slack water.

Name:	**G.B. Church**
Location:	Portland Island, B.C.
Position:	**48° 43.323' N 123° 21.339' W**
Depth:	**85'**
Access:	**Boat Dive**, Roche Harbor or West Beach Resort boat ramp.
Rating:	**Intermediate.**
Currents:	**West Point.**

History: The 175-foot long coastal freighter *G.B. Church* was built in Goole, England in 1943 and served in World War II as a supply ship for the allies in Europe. After the war, the ship was used for hauling explosives in and around British Columbia. She had originally been named the *Cerium* but was renamed by Bill Church after his father, George Bennett Church.

This delightful wreck dive was the very first project completed by the Artificial Reef Society of British Columbia. They successfully prepared and sank this ship on August 11, 1991 off of Portland Island in the Princess Margaret Marine Reserve near Sydney. For more information see their web site at artificialreef.bc.ca.

Dive Information: Today the *G.B. Church* rests upright on the bottom in very protected waters that are but a few miles from the San Juan Islands. The main deck is only about 50 feet below the surface and a white mooring buoy is attached to the forward mast which rises up to within 20 feet of the surface. Visiting divers from the U.S. can easily scoot over from Roche Harbor or West Beach, and in just a few minutes enjoy some spectacular wreck diving.

G.B Church

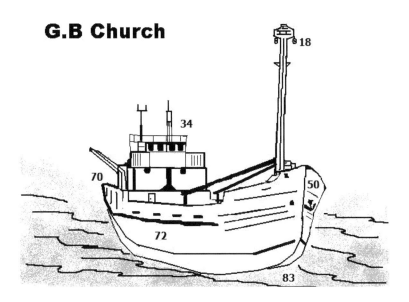

Huge ling cod and rockfish are found throughout the wreck which is in great shape. The Artificial Reef Society has thoroughly prepared this diver-friendly wreck with several access holes making this easy for all experience levels.

Notes: Charters operate out of Sydney or Victoria that regularly visit this artificial reef. If you're out in a private boat in the San Juans it would be a crime not to pop over and visit one of the best wrecks in the area. Recent underwater photos and more information about this wreck can be found by visiting northwestwreckdives.com. If you plan your visit to this wreck on a Sunday (as long as your neighbors don't see you pulling your boat out of the garage) you can say you spent the whole day at Church.

Cautions: Watch for boat traffic in the area, other divers, and pay attention to the current. It is generally very mild at this wreck, but it's a long swim home if you miss the boat!

Name:	**Gedney (Hat Island) Barges**
Location:	Everett, just off of Hat Island Marina
Position:	**48° 01.2437' N 122° 19.2679' W (northern)**
Depth:	**40-120'**
Access:	**Boat Dive**, ramp at Everett 5 miles east.
Rating:	**Intermediate.**
Currents:	**Possession Sound, weak and variable.**

History: Most likely sunk in service as a breakwater for the Hat Island Marina, these barges have no obvious markings or indicators as to what they were or where they came from. The remains of another barge was once visible on the beach to the south of the harbor.

Dive Information: These barges, scattered in disorderly fashion around the sea floor right below the Gedney Harbor entrance, are large and constructed of wood. They are the big oceangoing type with chain, deck gear, radar reflectors, and huge timbers to admire. They rise off of the bottom up to 20 feet and the deeper you dive the more intact they appear. The current is not bad here as the little bay provides just enough cover to diminish it. The bottom barge is nearly 120 feet deep, depending on the tide. The top barge is broken and scattered up the slope in as little as 40 feet of water.

Notes: Anchor your boat in shallow water (30 feet or so, remembering what depth you set your anchor) south of the harbor entrance and descend down your line. Follow the depth contour north at 70 feet until you hit the barges. For your return trip, follow the slope up until you reach the depth of your anchor and swim south until you run into it.

Gedney Reef is about 1.5 miles to the southeast which makes a nice alternate or second dive site to the *Gedney Barges*. However, the Reef is a little more current sensitive, so plan that dive around slack water. Gedney Reef coordinates are 47° 59.937' N, 122° 18.539' W in 30 – 60 feet of water.

Cautions: Surfacing directly from the barges is a very bad idea. If you are diving these wrecks, please use caution and dive as if you were in an overhead environment. Gedney Harbor is busy with boat traffic. The best of the barges are nearly beneath the entrance where boaters will be scanning the horizon for other boats, not an errant diver right in front of them. Keep an eye out for fishing gear, old line, old cables, and many other entanglement hazards that just love to catch on loose gauges or Jeff's new drysuit.

Name:	**Grace Foss**
Location:	Gig Harbor
Position:	**47° 20.0161' N 122° 34.8635' W**
Depth:	**40'**
Access:	**Boat Dive**, Gig Harbor Boat Ramp or Point Defiance ramps 3.4 miles east.
Rating:	**Beginner.**
Currents:	**Negligible.**

History: The fifty-five-foot long *Grace Foss* was a wood-hulled tug built in Astoria, Oregon in 1911. Originally named the *Ollile S*, she was moved to Seattle in 1918 and was renamed the *Rosedale*. The boat was sold to the Foss Tug Boat Company in 1927 and renamed the *Grace Foss*. The tug worked until sinking on December 14, 1954. She was raised and sold again to work as a passenger vessel around Lake Union until the tug sank for good in Gig Harbor in 1974 when her bilge pump failed.

Dive Information: Today there isn't much left of the old girl but her stern and propulsion machinery. They lie just off the end of the dock at Arabella's Landing where the *Grace Foss* sank at her mooring in 38 feet of water. Given the right access to the docks at Arabella's landing, this could easily be done as a shore dive. We did find a PVC table and a set of chairs near the wreck, so maybe it's a good place for a party?

Cautions: Gig harbor is well known for its boat traffic and although this wreck is not in the main channel like the *Burton,* it is right next to a working marina and busy docks. Try to dive this site in the winter when there isn't as much boat traffic and be sure to fly a dive flag to alert boaters in the area of the divers below.

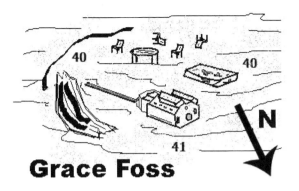

Grace Foss

Shore Diving with a GPS

For shore divers who want to use a GPS on the water, waterproof cases are available for handheld units. Just swim out to your dive site using it and then attach the GPS unit to your dive float, drop the small float anchor and enjoy your dive. This way you can swim right to the wreck without long navigation challenges. It is a perfect method for diving a wreck like the *Orca* from shore.

Note: We've come across a few divers searching for the wreck of the *Alida* in Gig Harbor. Although the *Alida* did sink in Gig Harbor and was shown on a few charts as still being there, she was in fact raised and salvaged.

Name:	Hauler
Location:	Atlantic City, Lake Washington
Position:	47° 31.5818' N 122° 15.0979' W
Depth:	100-120'
Access:	**Boat Dive**, ramps at Atlantic City ½ mile west or Gene Coulon Park 2 miles southeast.
Rating:	**Advanced,** due to depth, very low visibility.
Currents:	**None.**

History: The *Hauler* was located by Scott Christopher and John Sharps on September 30th, 2007 at the south end of Lake Washington.   The origins of this odd-looking vessel are unknown, but the aft-cabin design is very unique. This 65-foot long wood-hulled wreck was likely scuttled more than seventy years ago. It is located in the same general area as many other wrecks that were purposely sunk off of Atlantic City.

Dive Information: The *Hauler* is sitting upright on the silty bottom in about 120 feet of water. The roof of the generous aft cabin is missing. This makes it easy to drop inside and peer out the door, or the large, square windows into the dark lake.   The engine is in place below the main deck as are the well-built rudder and propeller beneath the rounded stern.

There is a sizeable forward deck area to explore in front of the cabin.   The deck hatch is missing, allowing access to the cargo and equipment areas for those divers trained and experienced in wreck penetration. Soft anchoring techniques should be used on this and all other wrecks in Lake Washington, to prevent damage to the old, soft wood.

Hauler

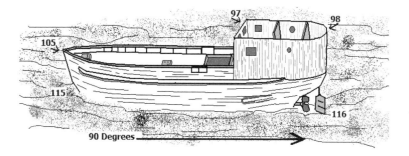

Notes: Many thanks to Scott and John for allowing us to publish this wreck so that others can enjoy the results of their hard work!

Cautions: This is a deep dive in a low visibility lake. Most would consider it a technical dive. You will find it very easy to get disoriented, lose your buddy, or lose the ascent line when diving in the dark depths of Lake Washington. Please do not attempt this dive until you have enough experience to be comfortable making a free ascent in the limited visibility water.

Bonus Dive

Name: **Atlantic City Scow**

Position: **47° 31.5256' N   122° 15.1481' W**

Depth: **110-120'**

History: The *Atlantic City Scow* was once a large motor-scow that had been converted to a barge before being sunk just 400 feet southwest of the *Hauler*. The wreck is fairly large and would make a good training site or an alternate dive if you happen to be in the area.

91

Name:	**Hildur Foss (aka Two Can Sam)**
Location:	Commencement Bay North, Tacoma.
Position:	**47° 17.7769' N 122° 25.8017'**
Depth:	**60-70'**
Access:	**Boat Dive**, ramps at Point Defiance 3.5 miles west or Redondo, 6 miles northeast.
Rating:	**Intermediate** due to visibility and silt.
Currents:	**Mild.**

History: The *Hildur Foss* was built at the Jensen Brothers Shipyard in Friday Harbor during 1907. She was originally named the *Venture* and served as a cannery tender along Puget Sound for many years. When the Wagner Towboat Company of Seattle was acquired by Foss in 1937, the tender was converted to a tug and the name was changed to *Hildur Foss*. Twelve years later she was scuttled in Commencement Bay on April Fool's Day, 1949.

Dive Information: The waters of Commencement Bay are very silty and the visibility is typically poor due to runoff from the Puyallup River. This dive may not appeal to everyone, but there is still a bit of the old wood hull poking out of the muddy bottom of the harbor. There are quite a few large steel tanks (fuel, water) lying along the port side of the wreck where they landed as the *Hildur Foss* deteriorated. Some of the deck machinery and a couple of interesting looking vents are the highlights of diving this old tug.

Hildur Foss

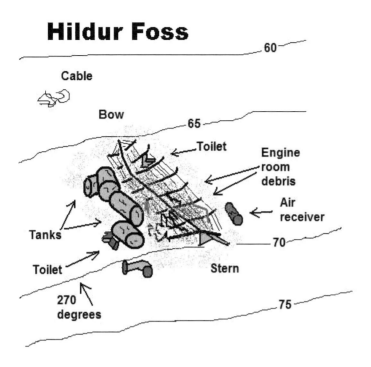

Notes: This may not actually be the *Hildur Foss*. It's hard to tell given the low visibility and deteriorated condition. The wreck is in the right location and is about the right age. We also thought that *Hildur Foss* is a much better name than our working title, which was "*Two Can Sam*" for the forward and aft toilets found in the debris. The wreck is located west of the barge storage area on the north side of the bay.

Cautions: This is an active harbor, so the best time to dive here is *not* during the peak of boating season. Try to pick a day after a fairly good dry spell in hopes of actually being able to see more than ten feet when you are at depth. Watch your fin techniques, as there is a thick layer of very fine silt covering the entire wreck site.

Name:	**Indianola Fishing Pier Wrecks**
Location:	Indianola Fishing Pier, Port Madison
Position:	**47° 44.629' N 122° 31.612' W**
Depth:	**40'**
Access:	**Boat Dive**, ramps at Kingston 3 miles north or at Shilshole 6 miles southeast.
Rating:	**Beginner.**
Currents:	**Port Madison, weak and variable.**

History: This boat has an interesting bit of local history. A retired Navy diver was a being a good Samaritan and offered to let a stranger he had just met tie his boat up for the night to a buoy he maintained off of Indianola. The next day the boat was still tied up but there was no sign of the owner.

A month later the diver received a call from the Keyport Naval Base that his boat was sinking. He rowed out to the boat and realized that it had been completely stripped with nothing left inside (including the hull ID plates). He did not want to leave the abandoned boat where it could be declared his responsibility or a hazard to navigation. He also knew that it would make a good fishing reef, so he rowed back out a couple of nights later with a few of bags of concrete and a drill and you can guess the rest. [Many thanks to Alan Buchanan for the real story.]

Dive Information: Diving the *Indianola Wreck* is a little like winning a three for one scratch off Lotto ticket. There are three wrecks all piled together on one little spot of sand, about 100 yards southwest of the end of the Indianola Fishing Pier. The larger wreck on the bottom looks like it was once a 40 foot, twin screw pleasure craft.

Indianola

Map by JC and
Nibbler Approved

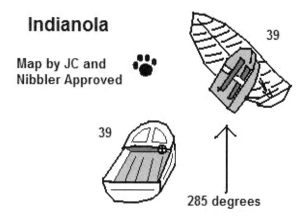

39

39

285 degrees

Notes: Since the sinking by our industrious Navy diver, someone has added a couple of small fiberglass (wee) wrecks to the wood-hulled cabin cruiser. The pile of wrecks lies in about 40 feet of water and makes a nice second dive after running through Agate Pass or diving the *Jefferson Head Minesweeper*.

Both of the propellers and rudders are still in place on the larger wreck as well as the large batteries, stuffing boxes, and propeller shafts that once pushed this boat around Puget Sound.

Cautions: If you are attempting this from shore, it is directly off the southwest end of the Indianola Fishing Pier. Swim out 350 feet on a heading of 200° magnetic from the SW corner of the pier and you should find the wrecks in 40 feet of water. Be aware that the fishing pier is very long and if you have to swim out and back from shore you're going to have a very, very long swim. There are often crab pots in the area. We spotted one stuck underneath the wreckage making it a minor entanglement hazard.

Name:	**Jefferson Head Minesweeper**
Location:	Jefferson Head, Puget Sound.
Position:	**47° 45.426' N 122° 28.166' W**
Depth:	**30'**
Access:	**Boat Dive**, ramps at Kingston 2.5 miles north or at Shilshole 5 miles southeast.
Rating:	**Beginner.**
Currents:	**Edmonds.**

History: The *Jefferson Head Minesweeper* was tied up and abandoned at the end of the Naval Degaussing Pier. A storm conveniently blew in and sank the wood-hulled vessel directly off the end of the dock. The pier is no longer there but the submerged piles can be found north of the wreck. This YMS class minesweeper was 136 feet in length and nearly twenty-five feet in width. With a displacement of 380 tons and a speed of about thirteen knots, she would have carried twenty-nine sailors during the war.

The degaussing station that previously occupied this site was used by the minesweepers to reduce their magnetic signatures. This made them less susceptible to the magnetically triggered mines that they were hunting.

Dive Information: The minesweeper rests in shallow water half a nautical mile north northeast of Point Jefferson (just off of Jefferson Head that the wreck is named for). Its location is well marked on NOAA chart #18446 (classic wreck symbol). The wreck is a little south of several submerged pilings that are also located on the same chart.

Jefferson Head Minesweeper

Stern

16

Fuel Tanks

25

Engine Mount

25

Sand/Silt

26

21

Tow Cable Spool

350 Degrees

Wires, Pipe and Hydraulic Hoses

Water Tank

25

26

Hydraulic Tank

22

Gantry

26

Bow

Most of the wood hull is gone but much of the deck rigging and machinery remains. There are also huge winches and a massive tripod that once supported the boom used for towing the minesweeping cable. Fuel and water tanks are still nestled inside the ribs of this coastal minesweeper. Large bitts that were once used for towing and sweeping for mines can be found in the sand.

Notes: This wreck is a very pleasant dive if you have access to a boat. Schools of striped perch like to follow divers around the wreck site, and we enjoyed looking at the bits and pieces and trying to guess what they were once used for.

Cautions: Try not to anchor on the north side of the wreck. There are several pilings from the old degaussing dock just below the surface of the water. This site is somewhat exposed to our typical southerly wind, so may it not be the best choice during small craft advisories.

Name:	**Kehloken, Possession Point Ferry**
Location:	Possession Point, south end of Whidbey Island
Position:	**47° 53.823' N 122° 23.591' W**
Depth:	**60-75'**
Access:	**Boat dive**, with ramps on Whidbey Island 6 miles north or Mukilteo 4.7 miles northeast.
Rating:	**Advanced** due to current.
Currents:	**Foulweather Bluff**, Puget Sound.

History: Built in 1926, the wood-hulled *Golden State* left the ship yard in 1927 for service in San Francisco Bay. In 1937 she was sold to the Black Ball Company, renamed *Kehloken* and used on the Puget Sound island ferry routes for years. In the 1950's traffic had increased to the point where the *Kehloken* became too small for major routes, so she was utilized as a utility ferry until her last run on Labor Day in 1972.

An infamous chapter in her history occurred when the ferry was used to take interned Japanese residents to Bainbridge Island camps in the early years (1942) of WWII. Eventually, she spent her own internment in Lake Washington until a fire burned her upper half in 1979. In 1983, using concrete slabs for extra weight, she was scuttled as an artificial reef/fish haven by the Department of Natural Resources. The concrete ballast is scattered in and around the wreck providing more habitat and an extra spot for divers to explore.

Dive Information: The *Kehloken* is a grand wreck that should serve as a case study on the benefits of artificial reefs. With the superstructure and car deck consumed in the fire, the wreck is open and inviting to the curious diver. The steel engine room structure and some machinery are still in place.

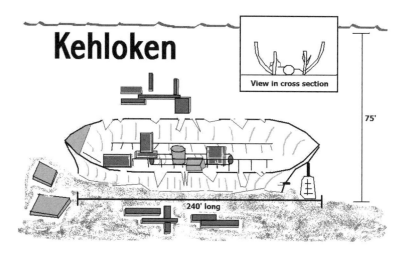

Kehloken

View in cross section

75'

240' long

The sides of the wreck rise up off the bottom eighteen feet and the entire area is covered with life. At 240 feet long and forty-four feet wide, she sits upright on the sea bed with no discernable list. The area around the wreck is very flat and averages 75 feet deep at mid-tide. The wreck lies in an east to west direction.

Notes: This ferry should be visited at different seasons in order to observe the ever changing creatures that inhabit the wreck throughout the year. High currents are common at this site so plan your dive around slack water and always have someone available in the boat. Anchoring directly on the wreck is possible.   We generally run a reel from the anchor up and over to the far side so that you can easily return to the boat no matter which side of the wreck you swim back on.

Cautions: You will find lots of fishing tackle, some lost and some still live. This is a very popular fishing spot so be aware that you may be sharing the wreck with fishermen. Try to improve the relationship between fisherman and divers. When given the opportunity, we frequently attempt to bring up a lost lure or stuck anchor for those fishing around the wreck.

Name:	**King Street Scow**
Location:	Lake Washington, Leschi
Position:	47° 35.714' N 122° 17.167' W
Depth:	20-30'
Access:	**Shore Dive**, enter at the end of King Street, swim out to 25 feet of water and turn right.
Rating:	**Beginner**, low visibility.
Currents:	**None.**

History: The *King Street Scow* is a wood-hulled barge that was abandoned and sank right off the end of King Street, south of Leschi Park in Seattle. There was once quite a bit of commercial activity and passenger ferry service in this area, but the floating bridge was built which put the ferries and barges out of work.

Dive Information: This shallow, easy to dive barge from a bygone era makes a good introduction to what diving is like in Lake Washington. Access to the site is very easy. Simply park at the end of King Street, gear up and climb down into the water. Swim straight out from the entrance path until you reach 25 feet of water, turn right (south) and swim until you run into the barge, which should only be a short distance away.

You will quickly discover that even though the light penetrates well at this depth, it is difficult to see very far. If you were to descend even deeper, you would quickly lose the light and the dive typically would become very dark at even sixty feet. The wood of this old barge is well preserved, and unlike diving saltwater wrecks you will not find much in the way of critters.

There will be the occasional crayfish, trout, perch, and other lake fish, but no colorful anemones will greet the visiting diver. If you explore the bottom around the barge carefully, you will often find artifacts from the heyday of the old steam ferries hiding among the more modern beer bottles and trash.

Notes: This isn't exactly the most exciting dive in Lake Washington (in fact it may be the least exciting). It is, however, a great place to get wet with easy access and a bit of interesting history to observe.

Cautions: Be sure to fly a dive flag to alert the boaters coming in and out of the docks near Leschi Park. Other than boaters and possible slippery rocks at the entry, this is a pretty benign dive site.

Many treasures lie buried at the bottom of Lake Washington, like the wreck of the Sonny.

Name: **HMCS Mackenzie**

Location: Gooch Island, Prevost Passage, San Juan Islands

Position: **48° 40.094' N   123° 17.170' W**

Depth: **60-75'**

Access: **Boat Dive**, Roche Harbor, Sydney or ramp at West Beach Resort on Orcas Island.

Rating: **Intermediate.**

Currents: **Turn Point, Boundary Pass.**

History: The *HMCS Mackenzie* was commissioned on October 6, 1962 in Montreal, Canada. She was just out of her sea trials when the Cuban Missile Crisis began, so she stayed on the East Coast for five extra months. From that point on she was a Pacific girl traveling to nearly 100 ports of call along the Pacific Rim before final decommissioning on August 3, 1993.

On September 16, 1995, the 366 foot *HMCS Mackenzie* began her second and longest career as an artificial reef. She is now a haven for sea life where she was intentionally sunk near Gooch Island, only two miles away from Turn Point in the San Juan Islands.

Dive Information: The *Mackenzie* is sitting upright on the bottom with a twenty degree port list that reminds you she is no longer a floating warship. This mild list is not severe enough to make orientation in and around the ship difficult. The bow is pointing west and is about 90 feet deep, but rises to nearly 50 feet at the top. The stern lies in 110 feet of water and the fantail is about 75 feet deep. The impressive 70 caliber guns greet you on the foredeck and the wheelhouse is a popular gathering place for divers visiting this fabulous wreck.

HMCS Mackenzie

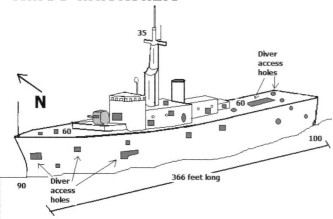

Prior to sinking, many holes were cut in the ship to allow divers access to key sections with numerous large exits. Still, wreck penetrations should only be done with proper training, experience, and equipment.

Notes: The Artificial Reef Society of British Columbia is an amazing group of dedicated people who work hard at providing wreck sites that are safe, fun, interesting, and actually very cool! For more information see their web site at artificialreef.bc.ca.

There is plenty of ship to see on such a large vessel. Plan to spend a couple of dives here and try to pick a day where the current is minimal. Alternate dives to the *Mackenzie* are the *GB Church* which is 4.2 miles northwest or Turn Point Wall, which is 2 miles to the northeast.

Cautions: There can be harsh currents at this site. Watch carefully and only dive when it can be done safely. Be sure to ascend on the same mooring buoy line that you descended. It is always a good idea to leave a capable driver in the boat to take care of your ride home and to keep a lookout for any divers who mess up their navigation.

Name:	Martha Foss

Location:	Dungeness Spit, Strait of Juan de Fuca

Position:	48° 08.243' N 123° 14.753' W

Depth:	45-55'

Access:	**Boat Dive**, ramps at John Wayne Marina in Sequim 14 miles east or Boat Haven Marina in Port Angeles 8.5 miles west.

Rating:	**Intermediate,** due to currents.

Currents:	**Angeles Point, very strong currents.**

History: The *Martha Foss* was a 96-ton steam tug that was built in Astoria in 1886. She was then converted to diesel and operated in northwest waters for the Alaskan Fish Salting and By-Product Company. The Foss Company purchased her on January 6, 1926 and kept her busy for the next 20 years.

On May 21, 1946 she collided with the ferry steamer *Iroquois* off of the Dungeness Spit, east of Port Angeles. The collision proved to be fatal to the aging tug and she began a quick trip to the bottom and then a slow ride into the sandy floor.

We are not entirely sure that this wreck is in fact the *Martha Foss*. The position from the collision is off by a short distance, and the size of the wreck seems to be too small. However, we did locate a diesel tug in the right area, so for now, we'll call her the *Martha Foss*.

Dive Information: The wood from this boat is all gone, but the machinery is there. At 55 feet of depth the wreckage is scattered over a small area and it is easy to make your way from one "item" to another. The bottom is flat and the only things that rise above it are parts of the wreck. Once you get your bearings, you will find many artifacts lying around. The layout will start to make sense and you can identify what each piece was before the barnacles and anemones moved in. The large diesel engine is often home to an octopus that hides underneath it like an old engineer trying to spark life back into the tired machine. The fenders, prop, reduction gear, and tail shaft are all here among the shells and sand.

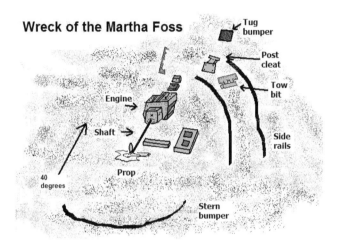

Wreck of the Martha Foss

Tug bumper
Post cleat
Tow bit
Engine
Shaft
Side rails
40 degrees
Prop
Stern bumper

Notes: This is really a fun wreck if you like to put the pieces of wreckage back together in your head. There is no hull left, but everything is where it should be and with a bit of imagination you can see how she was put together. It is close to the *Easy Eight*, and the *Dungeness Spit Crane*, so it makes a good second dive to the *Crane* and is a much better dive than the *Easy Eight*.

Cautions: There can be lots of current. This dive is in close proximity to the shipping lanes (it is just south of the west bound lanes). The bottom is not ideal for anchoring, as there are shells and small rocks that do not hold well. Be sure to check the set of your anchor before leaving for your dive. Like all high current sites, you should leave a qualified operator in the boat at all times.

Name:	**Maury Island Barges**
Location:	Maury Island, east side
Position:	**47° 21.746' N 122° 26.404' W**
Depth:	**35-65'**
Access:	**Boat Dive,** ramps at Redondo, 4 miles east or Point Defiance, 4.5 miles southwest.
Rating:	**Beginner.**
Currents:	**Mild, Blake Island.**

History: A cement company first developed the 80-acre gravel pit at this site in 1929. A large conveyor was built to load barges with gravel and many dolphins (clusters of pilings) were driven into the sea bed to hold the barges in place. Sometime in the late 1970's the conveyor was abandoned and three of the gravel barges that were tied to dolphins eventually sank due to neglect. They now provide a very nice recreational dive site that is easily accessible to many Central Puget Sound divers.

Dive Information: The three large gravel barges can be found roughly parallel to the dolphins on the south side of the conveyor. They sit upright and are in various stages of deterioration as the ship worms slowly win the battle with the wood structure of the barges.

Secure your boat between any two of the southern dolphins, descend at a piling and swim down slope a few feet to the wrecks. Observant divers will spot many varieties of fish and invertebrate life scattered throughout the site. Be sure to check the many cavern-like openings below the hull of the south barge, which is the one that is in the best condition. The pilings themselves also make for a very nice dive and are a great place to hang out on your safety stop.

Maury Island Barges

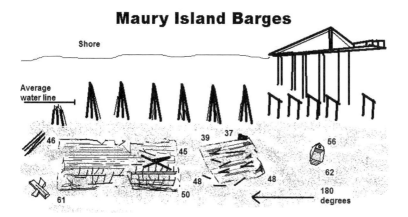

Shore

Average
water line

46
39 37
45
48
48
56
62
50
61
180
degrees

Notes: This site is very popular with charter operators and it is
not uncommon to see several boats tied up here at once. The site
is large and will accommodate numerous divers. The barges are
carpeted with lots of interesting critters. As a bonus, there is a
38 foot fiberglass boat sitting on the bottom just north of the
barges in about 55 feet of water near the conveyor.

Divers should not venture much further north than the small
fiberglass wreck. There is a large derelict vessel tied to the
dolphins north of the conveyor. Rumor has it that the occupant
of the *Cactus* is erratic and unpredictable, so there's no good
reason to dive there.

Cautions: This site is safe to dive during moderate tides, but
will see some current on a very large exchanges. Watch for
other divers when you approach by boat as this is a busy dive
site. Fly a dive flag and have a great time on one of the most
popular wreck dives in Central Puget Sound. Finally, if you do
want to actually see the barges, don't follow Scott's wife (Janet).

Name:	**Omar**
Location:	Seattle, just off of Shilshole Marina
Position:	**47° 40.393' N 122° 25.381' W**
Depth:	**65-80'**
Access:	**Boat Dive**, ramp at Shilshole 1 mile northeast.
Rating:	**Intermediate.**
Currents:	**Shilshole Bay.**

History: Prior to becoming a very cool dive site, the 65-foot wood-hulled *Omar* was employed as a tug boat from 1918 until she sank in Shilshole Bay due to neglect and heavy rains on November 12, 1995. Originally built in Greenpoint, New York, in 1918, she began her service for the Navy with a steam engine that was converted to diesel in 1934. She was sold to Simmons Tugboat Company in 1955 and worked out of Willapa Harbor for many years.

Dive Information: With a depth of about 80 feet to the sand and 65 feet at the deck machinery, this wreck isn't too deep for most divers. The *Omar* is in good condition and much of her deck gear is in place. There are a few holes in the hull around the sides and deck that fish like to peer out of. Many other creatures lurk just out of the light. There are lines running to the *Vertical* and *Horizontal Barges* from the *Omar*, but it is a long swim if you didn't bring your scooter!

The engine, smokestack, and towing winch reside on the deck along with a large hole near the bow that resembles the shape of the pilothouse. The propeller is long gone, but the large rudder offers an excellent photo opportunity.

Omar

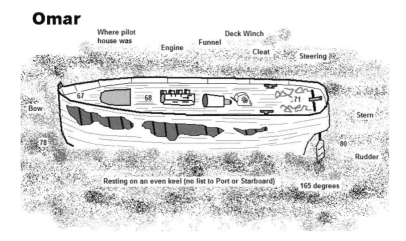

Notes: This wonderfully intact tug is one of the gems of the Seattle area. It is a popular site with charter operators as well as many boat divers due to its close proximity to Shilshole Marina and easy access. The *Omar* is also very close to the *Vertical Barge* and *Horizontal Barge* and diving all three wrecks makes for a great day under the water.

Making the long run between the tug and either of the barges is a good exercise in navigation. It is even more fun if you have the boat drop you off at one wreck and pick you up at the other. Nearby dive sites include the *Dauntless*, *Carkeek Park* and *Four Mile Rock Barges*.

Cautions: Large ships, tugs, and barges use the huge mooring buoy frequently. There are times when you will have to opt out of a dive here. Surfacing underneath a behemoth swinging in the wind or below a tug hooking up barges would make for a very bad day. There are many other fine sites close by, so you won't have to call it a day. Be sure to fly a dive flag and have a great time.

Name:	Orca

Location: Port Hadlock, Port Townsend Bay.

Position: 48° 02.028' N   122° 44.840' W

Depth: 55-65'

Access: **Boat Dive**, small boats can use the ramp at Port Hadlock 400 yards west or larger boats at Port Townsend 4.5 miles north.

Rating: **Beginner.**

Currents: **Negligible.**

History: The tug *Orca* sank at approximately 9 a.m. on September 20, 1999 at a mooring buoy about 2,000 feet north of Port Hadlock Marina. Wind pushed oil from the wreck into the marina causing a bit of a "stir" in the local newspapers. The tug was the smaller of two powerless vessels that had been removed from the Marine Science Center pier at Fort Warden State Park and secured to a mooring buoy off of Port Hadlock. The wind came up out of the north causing the *Orca* to sink unexpectedly. The larger barge that was tied up to it floated off into deeper water and sank.

Dive Information: The *Orca* rests in 65 feet of water, north of Port Hadlock Marina. Its location is well marked on NOAA chart #18464 (as a "WK" obstruction at the very south end of the map) and for a change, the charted position is spot on. This treasure, a 55-foot long tug, sits upright on the bottom and invites divers to come explore her. The bow points to the north and the towing bitts and windlass look as if they are ready for their next towing assignment.

Orca

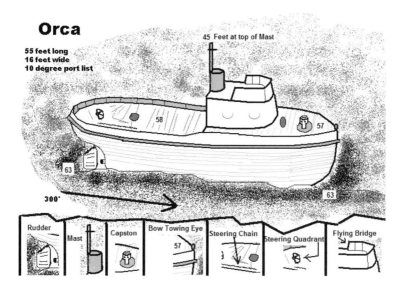

55 feet long
16 feet wide
10 degree port list

45 Feet at top of Mast

58

57

63

300°

63

Rudder	Mast	Capston	Bow Towing Eye	Steering Chain	Steering Quadrant	Flying Bridge
			57			

The controls on the flying bridge have collapsed into a jumble of wires and tubing, but the *Orca* is in remarkably good shape. Much of the blue paint still outlines the portholes on the cabin and the smoke stack, mast, and lights reach for the sun.

Notes: The steering quadrant and cables are exposed and give the visiting diver an interesting insight into how the tug's large rudder (which is still in place) was controlled while the *Orca* herded barges, logs, and ships into position at the docks she once worked.

This is a really pleasant dive on an intact tug. Visiting the *Orca* in conjunction with the *Alaska Reefer* to the north or the *Comet*, 400 yards to the west makes for a very enjoyable day on the water.

Cautions: This wreck is located outside of a working marina. Expect to see boat traffic going in and out of Port Hadlock. Fly a dive flag and keep someone on the boat if possible to ward off anybody approaching too closely.

Name:	**Owen Beach Barge**
Location:	Owen Beach, Point Defiance Park, Tacoma
Position:	**47° 18.8925' N 122° 31.7100' W**
Depth:	**90-100'**
Access:	**Shore Dive**, swim out directly in front of the picnic shelter, down slope to 95 feet, turn left and swim about 50 feet west to the barge.
Rating:	**Advanced,** due to depth.
Currents:	**Tacoma Narrows North.**

History: The history of the sinking of the barge at Owen Beach has been long forgotten. The wreck itself would normally not be popular were it not for the ease of access and the sixgill sharks that are often observed at this site.

Dive Information: The bottom at this site slopes steeply from 15 feet to about 110 feet. This wreck is very easy to navigate as the steep slope makes it simple to pick your depth and enjoy the dive. Enter the water below the west picnic shelter; swim down slope to 95 feet, then turn west (left) and swim a short distance to the barge.

The barge itself is a large steel frame about 100 feet deep on the north end and 85 feet deep on the shallow end. The decks have long since rotted away, but the healthy currents at this site have the wreck covered with marine life. We always find plenty of grunt and sailfin sculpins as well as octopus, gunnels, and a wide variety of fish.

Notes: The real draw for this particular dive site is the abundance of sixgill sharks in the area. The wreck provides a

very interesting macro dive to enjoy while you wait for the
sharks to show up and show up they do! We have been fortunate
enough to swim with and photograph sixgill sharks during
dozens of dives at this barge.

The best time to see sharks is late summer and early fall when
our plankton blooms make the water dark enough so that it does
not bother the primitive sharks' eyes. They never developed a
working iris to block out light. Take a slow cruise around the
barge, but keep an eye peeled behind you and out into the deeper
water.

Cautions: This is a fairly deep recreational wreck in a high
current area. Plan your dive so that you enter the water no more
than thirty minutes before slack at the Tacoma Narrows North
station. Remember to keep an eye on your gas supply and your
bottom time (especially when the sharks show up). Numerous
divers have unintentionally gone into mandatory decompression
at this site when they became carried away with shark
interaction. Simply head upslope when you are ready and take
your time as there is lots to see in the sandy gravel as you slowly
ascend to the surface.

Name:	**PBM Mariner**
Location:	Lake Washington, Renton
Position:	**47° 30.332' N 122° 12.819' W**
Depth:	**60-75'**
Access:	**Boat Dive**, ramps at Coulon Beach Park ½ mile east or at Atlantic City 2.3 miles northwest.
Rating:	**Intermediate.**
Currents:	**Negligible.**

History: On May 6, 1949 a U.S. Navy Martin PBM-5 was being towed across Lake Washington to the Boeing Seaplane Ramp at the south end of the lake when high winds caused a collision with a submerged object. The plane capsized and sank, after only being in service since 1944. It is now in the custody of the National Museum of Naval Aviation and no artifacts may be removed.

Dive Information: Although not a deep wreck by Lake Washington standards, it can get dark at this site. Visibility can be fickle so you may get an awful five feet or a refreshing twenty-five feet. The bottom is silty and thus easily stirred up. Whole sections of the plane can be obscured if one is not careful with fin techniques.

When descending onto the wreck it becomes obvious that this plane is massive, metal, and, unfortunately, upside down. The sheer size of the aircraft and the two very large engines are impressive. The propellers stretch to about 12 feet in diameter.

The wings are partially visible where they have been dug out of several feet of silt by the Navy during a salvage attempt. The tail was broken off during the last salvage effort and is now sitting in a museum. After breaking the tail off, the Navy was kind enough to install a mesh screen in the back of the aircraft to prevent unwary divers from penetrating into the body of the aircraft.

Notes: This is not a particularly glamorous wreck for critters or photo opportunities, but is awe inspiring by its size compared to many other aircraft wrecks. It is also very interesting because it was a flying boat and is definitely worth a visit if you're in the south end of the lake. It is also a good site for recreational divers to get a taste of what Lake Washington wreck diving is all about.

Cautions: Heavy boat traffic coming in and out of Gene Colon Park can be an issue, especially in the summer with jet skis buzzing about. Use caution and be sure to fly a dive flag.

Cockpit of the PB4Y bomber (see next page).

Name:	**PB4Y Privateer Bomber**
Location:	Lake Washington, Seattle.
Position:	**47° 40.5706' N 122° 14.4711' W**
Depth:	**150-160'**
Access:	**Boat Dive**, Magnuson Park ramp 700 yards west.
Rating:	**Technical.**

History: On August 26, 1956, a routine training flight from the Sand Point Naval Air Station went awry. The flight crew missed setting their flaps and the *PB4Y* Navy Bomber they were flying crashed into Lake Washington shortly after takeoff . The WWII bomber, a Navy version of the venerable B-24, sank in 175 feet of water after all crew were safely evacuated to life rafts. Salvagers eventually managed to get the plane back to the surface where a shackle pin broke and the aircraft sank back into the depths of Lake Washington. All further salvage efforts were abandoned.

The official Navy accident report lists the final position of the plane in 210 feet of water. The wreck seemed to be a forgotten bit of history lying undisturbed in the cold dark waters of the lake. Then the plane was rediscovered by divers and was found to be remarkably well preserved. It is resting on the muddy bottom in 155 feet of water, not far from the boat ramp at Seattle's Magnuson Park.

Dive Information: Going deep in Lake Washington can be extremely challenging. Visibility at depth generally runs about five to ten feet and the lack of contrast between the murky brown water and the muddy bottom has caused many a very experienced diver to "crash" into the mud on descent. This is often humorously described as watching their depth gauges go,

116

"120, 130, oops, where did the lights go," as they were enveloped by clouds of soft mud from the bottom.

All humor aside, descending and ascending in the gloomy waters can be disorienting. It should only be attempted by the most experienced technical divers who are very comfortable with near zero visibility at these depths. While this wreck would not seem that deep in the tropics, the pitch black, Braille-like conditions in the lake should be respected. There is no way I would dive this site without helium in my tanks and lots of deep diving experience, and hopefully neither would you.

Notes: The *PB4Y* (or the more modern name of *PBY*) is an impressive sight. The 110 foot wing span and massive Pratt and Whitney engines are in amazingly good condition. All six of the Browning 50 caliber machine guns are in place and the huge rudder and tail stand tall. The wreck is sitting upright with the starboard wing supported by the landing gear and the port wing supported by the bottom. The two large inboard engines were broken off in the salvage attempt, but the other two (and their massive propellers) remain in place.

All of the warning decals and signs on the aircraft are easy to read, including the 969 tail number. This makes the bomber look like it sank just a few years ago. The cockpit, instruments, and wheel are completely intact and are easy to observe through the open windows. The escape hatch on top of the aircraft speaks volumes to the retreat made by the crew.

Cautions: The Navy owns this aircraft and it is against the law to remove anything at all from the plane. Please take no artifacts from this monument so that future divers can enjoy the wreck as you do. Finding the machine guns and instrumentation in pristine condition are what makes this one of the best wreck dives in the Pacific Northwest.

Name:	**Phillip Foss**
Location:	Port Orchard
Position:	**47° 32.4542' N 122° 38.5910' W**
Depth:	**20-25'**
Access:	**Shore Dive**, from the small dock 400 feet southwest of the Water Street boat ramp.
Rating:	**Beginner,** very low visibility.
Currents:	**Weak and variable.**

History: What the *Phillip Foss* lacks in dive-site wonder it makes up for in rich history. She was originally built for the Red Salmon Canning Company and named after their Vice President (Frank B. Peterson). This tug hauled fish in Bristol Bay's Ugashik River in her holds and towed fish scows. In the winter she was moored at a company cannery in Alaska or in San Francisco.

In 1942 she was purchased by the Puget Sound Tug and Barge Company and her name was changed to *Lively*. Then in 1946 she was purchased by Foss and became the *Phillip Foss*. In February 1967 the old girl was damaged and subsequently retired. In August of 1968 she was towed to Port Orchard and anchored as a floating breakwater. While standing her last watch protecting the marina, she sank to the bottom where she lies today.

Dive Information: At a little over 20 feet deep (on average), this is an easy dive if you are comfortable with very low visibility. There are a few ribs, some wires and some other pieces of steel and cable strewn about, but most of this grand old tug has presumably sunk into the depths of the mud. Speaking of mud, this is the gooey smelly kind that only an African dung beetle would find fragrant (mmmmmm).

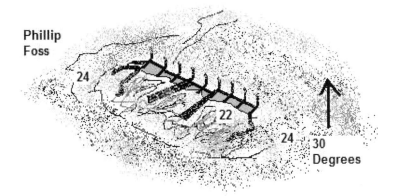

If you are actually crazy enough to try this dive from shore, walk out to the very end of the small dock that is located 300 feet west of the Water Street boat ramp. Jump in the water and swim due west about 100 feet before descending. This should put you right on top of the wreck. It may take a bit of searching due to the low visibility and the highly flocculated mud bottom. The silt is easily stirred up by an errant fin kick, so do watch your technique.

Notes: You know those dives that you can't wait to take a close friend to see? One of those special dives that is a must do? Well, this is one for someone whom you moderately dislike. After taking them here, they will likely not seek your company for many months afterwards. *Note from Scott , I took Jeff here and it didn't work!*

Cautions: This wreck lies in an active harbor. Stay close to the wreck; fly a dive flag and have a surface marker ready in case you don't ascend on a line or swim to shore.

Name:	**Prosper**
Location:	Port Angeles Harbor.
Position:	**48° 07.6735' N 123° 27.1782' W**
Depth:	**45'**
Access:	**Boat Dive**, ramp at Port Angeles 300 yards west.
Rating:	**Beginner.**
Currents:	**Negligible.**

History: The 45-foot long wood-hulled fishing vessel *Prosper* sank just outside of the entrance to the Port Angeles Boat Haven Marina in 1993. She most likely was abandoned at anchor and sank as the result of general neglect.

Dive Information: The *Prosper* rests upright in shallow water with a heading of 120°. The large fiberglass wheel house and deck structure have fallen off to the port side. There is an interesting stainless steel smoke stack protruding from the top of the cabin. There is also quite a bit of machinery and gear lying about the wreck including the mast and masthead lights along the east side.

The diesel engine, drive shaft, and rudder are in place inside the hull of the *Prosper* along with several fuel and water tanks. This boat once fished the waters of the Pacific Ocean. The location of this wreck is marked on NOAA chart #18468 (WK) and is less than 500 feet north northwest from the outer green marker at the entrance to the Boat Haven Marina.

Prosper

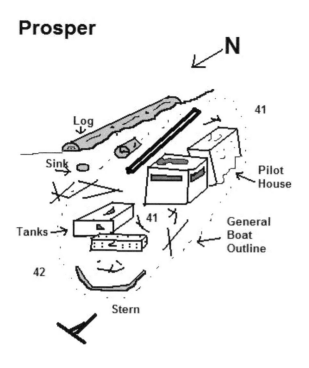

Notes: This wreck is an easy dive if you have access to a boat and could almost be done from the marina or ramp with scooters. Schools of striped perch like to follow divers around the wreck site and we enjoy looking at the bits and pieces of boat gear while trying to guess what they were once used for.

Cautions: With the location of this wreck being so close to the entrance of a working marina and a busy boat ramp, be especially cautious of recreational and commercial boat traffic. We usually dive these types of high traffic wrecks in the winter when there are very few boaters around. Be sure to fly a dive flag and to ascend on the anchor line so you don't surface in front of another boat. There are numerous entanglement hazards present on this wreck. Use caution so you don't accidentally swim into an overhead cabin in the low visibility.

Name:	**Puget Girl**
Location:	Port Angeles Harbor
Position:	**48° 08.102' N 123° 26.957' W**
Depth:	**80-85'**
Access:	**Boat Dive,** ramp at Port Angeles Boat Haven Marina ½ mile southwest.
Rating:	**Intermediate.**
Currents:	**Negligible.**

History: The 34-foot long, wood-hulled F/V *Puget Girl* sank in 1967 near Ediz Hook.

Dive Information: Plagued by poor visibility, this unremarkable wreck is easily forgotten. Visibility is often only five to ten feet in this part of Port Angeles Harbor's sheltered waters. The bottom is a light, fluffy silt that seems to puff up if you even think about using your fins. The wreck itself is nothing more than a little dory-sized wreck without a cabin. There are some old crab pot doors scattered around and some plumbing inside the wooden hull. A map of this wreck can be found on page 190.

Notes: If anyone is trying to hit all the wrecks in this book, you'll hate us for putting this one in. If you happen to already be diving inside the Hook and want to do one more, here you go. Have fun and don't worry about running into me on the bottom as I won't be going back anytime soon. If you are diving here, you might want to hit the *Prosper* which is a much better wreck.

Cautions: Large tugs anchor nearby in this busy harbor. Boat traffic can be dense, especially during fishing season. Fly a dive flag and have fun looking at the logs.

Name:	**Puget Sound El-Lame-O**
Location:	Eagle Harbor, Bainbridge Island
Position:	**47° 37.457' N 122° 30.235' W**
Depth:	**5-13'**
Access:	**Boat** or a really long swim from shore.
Rating:	**Beginner**
Currents:	**Negligible.**

History: AWOIS record number 52351 – "Located a deteriorating sunken boat." What an understatement! Just in case you thought the *Puget Girl* was the lamest wreck in the book, we had to add this one.

Dive Information: There are about six to seven inches of this boat sticking out of the sand about 15 feet south of the pilings. The highlight, by far, of this dive is the starboard stern where a bit of paint remains and a full seven inches of boat rises above the sand. On really good days, a barnacle might be feeding.

Notes: There are few books that concentrate only on wreck diving. Not one other publication comes right out and identifies the lamest wreck, but we will. This is, without a doubt, the worst wreck ever and a complete waste of your time. The only reason it is here on this page, besides making the second worst wreck seem a bit better, is that we don't want you to find some literature that says there is a wreck here and then you waste your time trying to find it like we did (map on page 191).

Cautions: The only real danger at this site is utter and complete boredom and the great Pacific, glove-eating barnacle on the starboard quarter of this useless excuse for a wreck.

Name:	**Quartermaster Wreck**
Location:	Quartermaster Harbor, Maury Island.
Position:	**47° 20.9888' N 122° 29.0152' W**
Depth:	**65-75'**
Access:	**Boat Dive**, ramps at Point Defiance 2.8 miles south southwest or Redondo 5.3 miles east.
Rating:	**Beginner.**
Currents:	**Gig Harbor entrance.**

History: This unknown 57-foot wood-hulled fishing boat was scuttled near the entrance to Quartermaster Harbor. The wreck was loaded with old engine blocks, air receivers, fans, and concrete culverts from a nearby shipyard and then sunk out in the middle of the channel. The wheelhouse is missing, but the outline and paint are visible showing where an attractive round front cabin once stood. The grey-blue trim, red bottom and white painted sides stand eleven feet off the bottom with the hull and deck largely intact. The engines, machinery, rudder and propeller are in place.

Dive Information: The bottom offers good anchorage, but please try to anchor to either side of the wreck so as not to damage it. One local charter operator has already dropped a large anchor through the back deck of the wreck. You won't find them on our list of recommended charters any time soon.

The bow of the *Quartermaster Wreck* still points due south, right at Old Tacoma. This makes navigating the wreck quite easy, but there is often poor visibility in the harbor. Be prepared for the worst and pleasantly surprised when you catch a good day. There are usually lots of pregnant rockfish and several varieties of nudibranchs hanging out in the holds.

Notes: The *Quartermaster Wreck* is located about 1000 feet west northwest of the red Manzanita buoy, right in the middle of the channel at the entrance to Quartermaster Harbor (between Maury and Vashon Islands). It is well protected from most winds and makes a great second dive after Dalco Wall or the *Maury Island Barges*. The wreck shows up quite easily on a fish finder with lots of vertical structure. When anchoring, wait until the structure just drops off to lower your anchor next to the side of the wreck. This will make the dive pleasant and recovery of your anchor much easier. You will find the map for this wreck on page 190 along with the story of the golden coins that we found inside (page 182).

Cautions: This is really not a current sensitive dive site, but is in a high traffic area, so be sure to display a dive flag and pick a time with minimal boat traffic. Diving this site in the summer when crab season first opens is probably not such a good idea.

Name: Ranger

Location: Port Townsend.

Position: 48° 06.2707' N   122° 46.5893' W

Depth: 15-35'

Access: **Shore Dive**, just outside the breakwater at the Boat Haven Marina in Port Townsend.

Rating: **Beginner.**

Currents: **Marrowstone Point northwest.**

History: The *Ranger* was being refitted or salvaged in the marina when it was moved to the old ferry dock. There it was abandoned and allowed to sink. The wood-hulled work boat is about 70 feet long and is constructed of very stout timbers and large iron spikes.

Dive Information: The *Ranger* lies just off the breakwater around the Boat Haven Marina in Port Townsend. It is accessible from shore, located in about 30 feet of water near the old railroad ferry terminal west of the marina.

When the boat sank, she took out many of the pilings at the ferry dock's west wing wall. She now sits upright on the bottom, hard against and on top of the old wing wall. This makes finding the *Ranger* pretty easy--just follow the wing wall heading northeast from the old railroad ferry terminal. Her deck is only about 15 feet deep and she is easily visible from the surface.

This wreck is very large and is covered with many varieties of nudibranchs. For those nerd-like (i.e., Jeff) wreck divers, the chain steering pulley and cables which once controlled the huge rudder to maneuver this big boat around Admiralty Inlet are

visible. The propeller is long gone and so is the wheel house.
Bits and pieces of machinery and hardware can be found hiding
around the vessel.

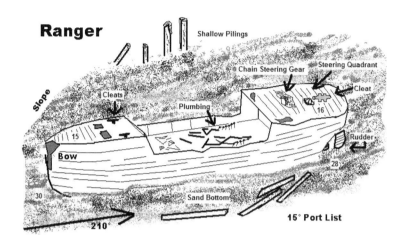

Notes: To access the *Ranger* from shore, park near the restroom
at the shipyard southwest of Boat Haven Marina in Port
Townsend. Gear up and walk, wade, or swim to the wing wall of
the old railroad ferry dock. The dock is plainly visible with
many sections between the shore and the old ferry slip collapsed
or removed. Once at the wing wall (there is only one), swim to
the end of the visible piles, then continue northeast following the
line of submerged piles. You'll spot the *Ranger* on the bottom
about 100 feet north of the ferry dock.

Cautions: The broken off pilings near the wreck are mostly
submerged, but dangerous if diving this site by boat. Be aware
that once the visible pilings end, the broken off pilings continue
along the same lines and are lurking just below the surface of the
water.

Name:	**Reid Harbor Wreck**
Location:	Reid Harbor, Stuart Island
Position:	**48° 40.127' N 123° 11.243' W**
Depth:	**25-30'**
Access:	**Boat Dive,** Roche Harbor 4 miles south southeast or West Beach Resort 9.5 miles east.
Rating:	**Beginner.**
Currents:	**Negligible.**

History: Nothing is known about the history of this wreck.

Dive Information: This wooden hulled boat is nearly broken down and looks as though it is now part of the silt at the bottom of Reid Harbor. There is only about two feet of relief off the bottom at its highest point. The wreck is hard to find due to the poor visibility that plagues this small harbor.

Notes: For those of you who are compelled to dive it, there is an old steering armature along with some boat equipment near the stern and a few undiscovered relics in the silt around the wreck. Reid Harbor is located at Stuart Island in the San Juans. This island is also the location of the best wall dive in the Pacific Northwest (Turn Point Wall). The only reason to dive this site rather than Turn Point Wall or Charles Point would be howling winds and exceptionally nasty weather. The area is very well protected, but pretty boring unless you're a wreck nut like Jeff.

Cautions: Visibility is typically five feet or less and once you stir up the silt, you will be in zero-vis. If you do get silted out, just go up a few feet and the visibility will improve.

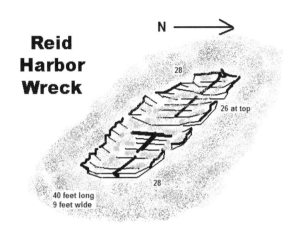

Reid Harbor Wreck

N ⟶

28

26 at top

28

40 feet long
9 feet wide

Anchor windlass of the G. B. Church.

Name:	**Point Richmond Minesweeper**
Location:	Point Richmond, Colvos Passage
Position:	**47° 23.250' N 122° 32.920' W**
Depth:	**60-65'**
Access:	**Boat Dive,** ramps at Gig Harbor 4 miles south or Point Defiance 5 miles south.
Rating:	**Beginner.**
Current:	**90 minutes before Tacoma Narrows North.**

History: The *Point Richmond Minesweeper* is an unknown 160-foot long wood-hulled vessel that was sunk at the site of an old shipyard/salvage operation. The vessel is commonly referred to as a minesweeper (due to the wood hull), but the remains are so scattered across the bottom that it is hard to tell. The ribs and debris stand about five feet off the bottom. The engines, machinery and propeller have all been removed, but interesting bits and pieces of the wreck can still be found including the bath tub, cabinets, and even an occasional dish.

Dive Information: The location of this wreck, just north of Richmond Point, is fairly current sensitive. If you are running a live pickup boat, drop in at 60 feet off of the first of five pilings, whichever is up current. Then let the current carry you right to the wreck. The bow points due north making navigation very easy. The currents in the area bring nutrients to an amazing variety of creatures that make their home on the wreck-turned-reef. Nudibranchs, crabs, and sea stars crawl about looking for their next meal. Rockfish peer out at divers from holes in the wreck while a forest of anemones feast on the jellyfish that are swept into their midst.

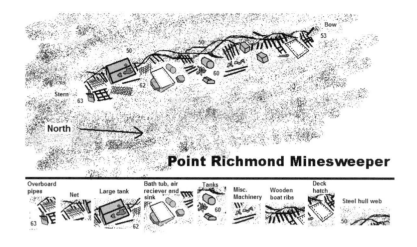

Point Richmond Minesweeper

Notes: The wreck is easy to locate between the second and third set of pilings (from the north) at about 65 feet of depth. Anchor the boat during slack water or take turns diving the wreck during mild currents. You'll be rewarded with a nice dive showcasing how Mother Nature turns an old wreck into a lovely garden.

Cautions: There is a bit of rotting net scattered near the stern of the wreck so be careful and carry a sharp dive knife with you. Richmond Point is a popular fishing spot. Don't let the current carry you too far south before surfacing or you might become part of a good fishing story about the "one that got away".

If you are interested in making your diving safer, drinking lots of water to keep yourself well hydrated is one of the easiest ways. Drink some water before your dives and again right after you finish. Unfortunately, beer does not really make for a well hydrated diver. Don't drink and dive.

131

Name:	**Salt Water State Park Barge**
Location:	Salt Water State Park, Des Moines
Position:	**47° 22.403' N 122° 19.687' W**
Depth:	**30-45'**
Access:	**Shore Dive**, enter at Salt Water State Park and swim out to the large white buoy.
Rating:	**Beginner.**
Currents:	**Tacoma Narrows North.**

History: The wooden gravel barge that is located on the bottom in front of Salt Water State Park was sunk as an artificial reef in 1971 by the Washington State Department of Fisheries. The ship worms have reduced the large barge to a scattered reef. A few ribs, vents, valves and other machinery provide plenty of habitat for a wide variety of fish and invertebrates.

Dive Information: To locate the barge from shore, swim out due west from the foot of the concrete steps to the large cylindrical orange and white buoy that marks the location of the wreck. The wreck was once surrounded by a field of old tires. As you explore the bottom, finding tires usually means you have swum past the end.

Salt Water State Park is a fairly busy site, so expect to share it with other divers in the area. It is a long surface swim out to the barge (~ 150 yards). Take a break to catch your breath once you arrive and then descend into an underwater garden of interesting marine life.

Salt Water State Park Barge

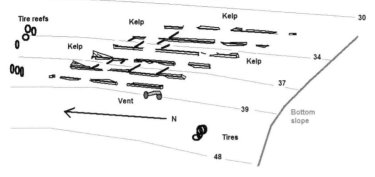

Notes: This is a good site for macro photography. There is almost always a good selection of nudibranchs, shrimp, and other small critters that are willing to pose for the aspiring underwater photographer. Take your time as you swim slowly around the ribs and wreckage of the barge and you are almost sure to be rewarded by the sight of a rare and photogenic creature to add to your collection.

The tire reefs aren't the best marine habitat in the world and may have been removed by the time you read this. You do occasionally find something interesting, like an octopus or ling cod with eggs that take up temporary residence on the reef.

Cautions: The park can get crowded on sunny days which can make finding a parking spot the most challenging part of the dive. This can lead to a long walk to the water with your gear, and then you face the long surface swim out to the barge. The current can get unmanageable at this location during large tidal exchanges. It is best to plan your dives around slack water in the Narrows, entering the water up to an hour before predicted slack.

133

Name:	**Seahurst Park Barge**
Location:	Seahurst Park, Burien
Position:	**47° 28.841' N 122° 21.932' W**
Depth:	**35-45'**
Access:	**Shore Dive**, enter at Seahurst Park.
Rating:	**Beginner.**
Currents:	**Weak and variable.**

History: The wooden barge at Seahurst Park was used by the Army Corps of Engineers to transport the dismantled seawall out of the park in 1972. It was then used to bring in nearly 15,000 tons of sand and gravel to build up the park's shoreline after the seawall removal. Once the project was completed the barge was sunk as fish habitat.

Dive Information: To locate the barge from shore, swim out from the lower parking lot heading northwest until you are at 40 feet of depth. Turn north and follow the 40-foot contour until you find the scattered wreckage. It has been reduced to broken ribs sticking up several feet from the sandy bottom along with many vent pipes and a few bits of bilge plumbing.

To locate the barge visually from the surface, line up the two poles from the "doughnut sculpture" (you'll know it when you see it) with 40 feet of water (nearly 1000 feet off the beach). The hard parts are covered with anemones, sponges and the nudibranchs that eat them. Bring a camera and keep a sharp eye out for those elusive critters.

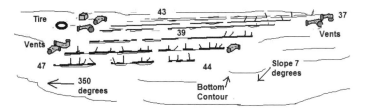

Seahurst Park Barge

Notes: The wreck is a long, long swim out from shore so we prefer to dive this site from a boat. Those of you that like long scooter dives might find this to be a fun challenge.

Do keep an eye out in the eelgrass beds above the barge as there is always lots to see if you pay attention. On our last visit to this site, there was a white and blue mooring buoy located about 100 feet inshore. If the buoy is still in place, you should be able to locate the wreck easily by swimming to the buoy and then heading down slope to about 40 feet of depth.

Cautions: Seahurst Park can get very crowded on weekends. Finding a parking spot is almost as challenging as the walk to the water at low tide and the long swim out to the wreck. The current tends to be pretty mild and the site can be safely dived on all but the largest tidal exchanges.

> Gear maintenance is critical for divers who are entering a harsh environment where they normally cannot survive. We rely on our equipment to keep us safe. This in not the place to re-use an old o-ring or to skimp on a regulator that is sticking a bit, thinking that it will be okay for a couple more deep dives before you have it serviced. It's your life—Take Care!

Name:	**Shilshole Barges (Vertical and Horizontal)**
Location:	Seattle, just off of Shilshole Marina
Positions:	**47° 40.4300' N 122° 25.3567' W horizontal**
	47° 40.3767' N 122° 25.3183' W vertical
Depth:	**50-90'**
Access:	**Boat Dive**, ramp at Shilshole 1 mile northeast.
Rating:	**Intermediate.**
Currents:	**Shilshole Bay.**

History: The large yellow mooring buoy that marks the location of the *Shilshole Barges* is one that has been used for years as a staging area prior to moving barges into and out of Lake Washington.   The wrecks sank due to differential loading while moored and waiting to be rafted. It appears that they sank sometime in the last thirty to fifty years.

Dive Information: The *Vertical Barge* is unique and a wonderful dive. It is lying on its port side and is almost straight up and down. One of the most impressive things about this steel beast is that it has not fallen over. It must have been perfectly placed so as not to face any kind of current. Even a tiny bit would be enough to push it over. The barge rises forty feet off the bottom and is covered with marine life. You can swim from one end to the other and return on the upper edge (starboard side) on your way back for a great dive. The very deepest part rests in 90 feet of water.

The *Horizontal Barge* is also in 90 feet of water (map in appendices). It is bigger than the *Vertical Barge* and it is lying on an even keel. It takes a full dive to circumnavigate and to cover the deck. One side looks just like the other, so don't feel as though you're cheating if you skip anything. The bulwarks, cleats, forward light mast, and the deck gear are interesting.

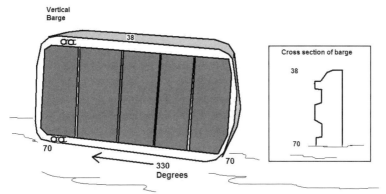

Notes: There are guidelines that run between the two barges and the *Omar.* Don't go down the lines expecting a short swim. With three great wrecks to visit at this site, you can make a full day here and still be close enough to shore that you can slip in for a mocha between dives. There is a lot to see and plenty of room for numerous dive groups.

The wreck of the *Omar* lies closest to the giant yellow mooring buoy. The *Horizontal Barge* is about 200 feet due north of the *Omar* (350°) in 90 feet of water. The *Vertical Barge* is about 200 feet southeast of the *Horizontal Barge* (120°).

Cautions: There is no reason to penetrate any of these wrecks. Plan your dive so that you have enough air to come back to your anchor where you can make a safe ascent to the surface.

These wrecks lie just off the entrance to the Ballard Locks; therefore, there is a lot of boat traffic in the area. Keeping a competent captain to watch out for the other boats is always a good idea. Be sure to fly your dive flag and have fun.

Name:	**Snickerdoodle**
Location:	Atlantic City, Lake Washington
Position:	**47° 31.350' N 122° 15.622' W**
Depth:	**25'**
Access:	**Boat Dive**, ramp at Atlantic City, 700 feet northwest.
Rating:	**Beginner.**
Currents:	**None.**

History: Obviously scuttled, this diminutive wood-hulled tug is very cute, but her origins remain to be discovered. It was named by the authors for a very tasty cookie we were eating when we found it. We were towing a distressed vessel in off of the lake when we spotted this delightful dive on the side scan.

Dive Information: At a depth of only 25 feet this interesting little wreck is photogenic and fun. There are a few barrels in the bilges and some old steel portholes that decorate the bulwarks. A small row boat rests off the stern and a few pieces of equipment remain bolted to her ribs.

Notes: The *Snickerdoodle* is probably the most picturesque wreck in the lake with light streaming down from the surface. There doesn't seem to be as much silt as you might find at other Lake Washington wrecks.

The odd looking object located in the mud on the west side of the wreck is an old outboard motor cover that some boater probably lost while wrenching on his poor old Johnson.

Snickerdoodle

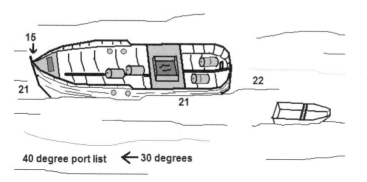

15
↓
21
22
21

40 degree port list ⬅ 30 degrees

Cautions: Boat traffic can be dangerous here as the wreck is located very close to a working marina and a busy boat ramp. Wise divers will keep a person aboard their boat to wave a dive flag in order to warn off unaware boaters. This wreck is best to dive outside of peak boating season.

The Snickerdoodle Tug

Name:	Sognefjord
Location:	Neah Bay
Position:	48° 22.657' N 124° 36.336' W
Depth:	20-30'
Access:	**Boat Dive**, ramp at Neah Bay ¾ mile southwest.
Rating:	**Beginner.**
Currents:	**Negligible.**

History: The *Sognefjord* was a thirty-seven foot long fishing boat that sank in Neah Bay in 1983 after catching fire in the harbor. The fiberglass hull now sits forlornly on the bottom in thirty feet of water and is pretty much all that remains of this hard working boat.

Dive Information: The bottom at this site is flat and muddy, so the visibility here is usually pretty poor. The wreck itself is completely covered with fishing nets which can be an entanglement hazard if you're not careful. The twin propellers and rudders are still in place which makes the stern the most interesting part of this wreck dive. The middle of the boat is filled with silt (and nets), and it takes a sharp eye to make out the subtle features below the deck.

If you are bored here, there is an equally uninteresting rock wall to explore just to the east of the wreck. It is called The Uninteresting Rock Wall Just East of The Wreck. It seems to be a popular place to hang out if you are a juvenile rockfish or a lonely anemone, but your chances of seeing another diver here are very low, unless you brought them with you.

Sognefjord

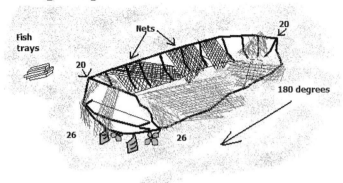

Notes: There are much, much better dive sites just on the other side of Waddah Island from this wreck. However, if you're stuck in the harbor, waiting on inclement weather, the *Sognefjord* and *Western Anchor* wrecks might keep you amused for a short while. It is an easy wreck to find. Just drag a net around and you will inevitably hang it up on the stern. That is how several boats have located it so far, but you can also use more traditional methods like a depth sounder.

There seems to be a strong magnetic disturbance here that can pull drysuit zippers slightly open. Wetsuits and Jeff's particular brand of drysuit seem to be unaffected, but Scott's had trouble. When the magnetic disturbance is active, it sounds very much like a muffled high pitched scream under water.

Cautions: Lots of fishing nets completely cover this fiberglass hull. Stay out of the nets and you should be "good to go" on this easy wreck dive. Boat traffic is improbable, but you can never be sure. Fly a flag here as yachts will sometimes anchor in the bay. The boat ramp at Neah Bay is narrow and the courtesy dock is dilapidated, but serviceable.

Name:	**Sonny**
Location:	Lake Washington, Rainier Beach
Position:	**47° 31.3639' N 122° 14.9249' W**
Depth:	**110-120'**
Access:	**Boat Dive**, ramps at Atlantic City ½ mile west or Gene Coulon Park 2 miles southeast.
Rating:	**Advanced,** due to depth, very low visibility.
Currents:	**None.**

History: The origins of the wreck of the fishing vessel *Sonny* are unknown, but it is a very pleasant dive back into history. The 38-foot wood-hulled vessel is remarkably well preserved by the cold, dark waters of Lake Washington. Located at the south end of the lake in only 120 feet of water, it is also a fairly easy dive as far as dives in the lake go.

Dive Information: The *Sonny* stands proud and upright on the bottom of the lake. Her propeller and engine are in place, as is some of her deck machinery. The rudder moves easily to the touch and a large fishing boom lies off to the port side. The aluminum wiring on the boom is quite old, with some type of canvas or cloth insulation.

Note from Scott: On my first dive here, I thought the wheelhouse was so picturesque that I decided to forego diving another wreck in order to return to the Sonny to get some photos. The floor of the wheelhouse had collapsed, exposing the engine, transmission, and running gear below. Just aft of the wheelhouse, a power driven hoist once pulled heavy items up and down the boom.

Inside the wheelhouse of the Sonny

Notes: The *Sonny* looks a lot like a tug, but the only large bitt is forward of the cabin. The large boom indicates she was used for hauling nets or something similar at one point in her career. The name of the vessel is faintly visible on the starboard bow and the rails are now lying over on their sides.

Cautions: This is a deep dive in a low visibility lake. Many would consider it to be a technical dive. It is very easy to get disoriented, lose your buddy, or lose the ascent line when diving in the dark depths of Lake Washington. Please do not attempt this dive until you have enough experience to be comfortable making a free ascent in the limited visibility water.

This wreck is located near several busy marinas, so watch out for boat traffic. Fly a dive flag and be sure to leave a qualified captain on the boat. Have a great time on a remarkable wreck.

Name:	**Steele Dodge Sedan**
Location:	Ambulance Point, Lake Crescent
Position:	**48° 03.422' N 123° 52.874' W**
Depth:	**195-200'**
Access:	**Shore Dive,** entry east of Meldrim Point.
Rating:	**Technical, due to depth.**

History: On January 24, 1960, Highway 101's Ambulance Point claimed another vehicle when Dale Steele's 1950 Dodge sedan slid off the icy road into the dark depths of the lake. Beverly Sherman was a passenger in the back seat and was only 20 years old at the time of the accident. All four passengers in the car swam to safety and watched the dimming headlights descend into the inky blackness of Lake Crescent. Forty-four years later Beverly read about the discovery of the *Warren Wreck* in the lake and contacted the dive team to see if they could locate Steele's car to recover her suitcase from the trunk.

In 2004 the old Dodge was located and Sherman's suitcase full of memorabilia was recovered and returned to her. Today, the *Steele Dodge* is located in 200 feet of cold, clear water not far from the *Warren Wreck* which sank in 1929. The car sits on the edge of a steep ravine facing up the cliff-like slope. The vehicle is wedged in amongst some old trees and branches which gives it a bit of an eerie look!

Dive Information: Locating the *Steele Dodge* is fairly straight forward. Enter the water at the turnout just east of Meldrim Point (aka Ambulance Point) and descend straight down slope in the chute. Once you reach 190 feet, look to your right. The car sits on a slight hump on the hillside at 195 feet of depth. The clear, cold waters of the lake make this a chilly but pleasant dive. You can still see blue water and visible light even at this depth.

Notes: Diving the *Warren Wreck* requires a permit from the National Park Service. This may not be necessary when diving the *Steele Dodge*, but be sure to get a permit if you plan to dive both wrecks.

Scootering from this wreck to the *Warren Wreck* is very popular and works well, but they are much too far apart to even consider a swim at these kind of depths. Spending ten minutes or so at this wreck and then traversing with a scooter to the other wreck at 170 feet is a lot of fun and makes for a great dive plan.

Cautions: The depth of this old sedan is well beyond the limits of recreational diving, so be sure you have the appropriate training and experience before tackling this spectacular dive. The impressive wall structures of the ravine that you drop through are worth the dive, even if you didn't have an interesting wreck to look at. Be safe and have a great time on a fascinating historical artifact.

Name:	**Steilacoom Marina (aka Saltar's Point)**

Location:	Saltar's Point Park, Steilacoom.

Positions:	47° 10.121' N	122° 36.838' W	**Fishing Boat**
	47° 10.101' N	122° 36.833' W	**Piling Wreck**
	47° 10.073' N	122° 36.862' W	**Hatch**
	47° 10.050' N	122° 36.860' W	**Cooper**
	47° 10.044' N	122° 36.820' W	**Holland**
	47° 10.072' N	122° 36.889' W	**Chris Craft**

Depth: 20-30'

Access: **Shore Dive**, enter via Saltar's Point Park.

Rating: **Beginner.**

Currents: **Negligible.**

History: There are at least six wrecks located out in front of the old Steilacoom Marina which is also known as Saltar's Point. The murder of the marina's owner in 1988 is a sad part of Pierce County history. It put thirteen year old Barry Massey in prison for life (without parole) and led to the demise of the once colorful and thriving marina as well as shattering the lives of the owner's family.

Dive Information: For boat divers (and shore divers) there is easy access to these wrecks via Saltar's Point Park which is south of the Steilacoom Ferry dock at Gordon Point. One of the wrecks, which was once a commercial fishing boat, is located right out in front of the picnic shelter in only 25 feet of water. Swim further south in 30 feet of water and you'll find the *Pilings Wreck* lying against the northernmost piles from the old Steilacoom Marina. This small day cruiser sits with her bow pointing east where she had been moored prior to sinking.

Steilacoom Marina

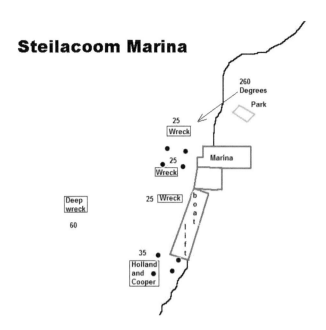

Just a bit further south, probably 75 feet away and about eight feet shallower is the broken remains of the 20 foot long wreck we call the *Hatch*. She was named for the deck hatch that lies in the middle of the wreck (its most remarkable feature).

The best of the wrecks are all of the way to the south and lie together in between the cluster of southern pilings. The *Cooper* is a day boat similar to the *Piling Wreck* and sits in about 30 feet of water. She is wedged in between the deep south piling and the *Holland*.

The *Holland* is a small utility tug complete with a tiny towing bitt, prop, and rudder. It is interesting to note that the metal framework that once ringed the deck and held the mast has been pulled free and is lying along the starboard side. There is also a small windlass and cleat on the bow as well as a hollow where the pilot house once sat.

The deeper wreck appears to be an older *Chris Craft*. It is in good condition in 60 feet of water just to the north of the *Holland* and *Cooper*. The construction style of this wreck will remind you of the boats of yesteryear and is certainly one of the highlights of diving this site. (See maps on page 188.)

Steilacoom Marina South

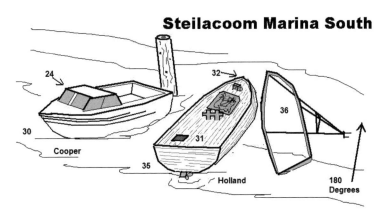

Notes: Finding these wrecks is fairly straightforward. Swim along at the target depth and follow that contour until you run into the wreck. A buddy team can spread out a couple of feet to cover a wider depth range to help account for tidal fluctuation.

Piling Wreck

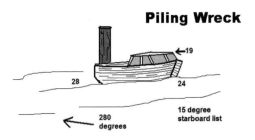

Cautions: This marina could see some activity. There are still boats in the slings above the water and kayakers are nearly always around on the beautiful days. Boat traffic and fishing are likely here, so fly a dive flag and watch out.

Name:	**Stella**
Location:	Steilacoom, Sunnyside Park
Position:	**47° 10.7385' N 122° 35.4935' W**
Depth:	**40'**
Access:	**Shore,** enter via Sunnyside park.
Rating:	**Beginner.**
Currents:	**Negligible.**

History: The *Stella* (named after Steilacoom) is another wee wreck of convenience. It has been handily placed here and ours is not to question why. This wreck is an old twenty-four foot fiberglass boat with an interesting stern design.

Dive Information: Located in front of Sunnyside Park at Steilacoom, this wreck lies on a sandy bottom and is sitting upright, facing shore. Visibility is generally good and the sand is forgiving of divers that get too near the bottom and stir things up a bit. Enter the water at the pilings in front of the rest rooms and you will find the Stella about 80 yards from shore on a 250° (magnetic) heading in forty feet of water.

Notes: The *Stella* is a photogenic little wreck and anyone with a small underwater camera should be able to get some good buddy shots for that Christmas card you always wanted to make.

Cautions: Boats do come by and are sometimes dropping passengers off or picking them up from the beach. Fly a dive flag and surface near it or swim underwater to the shallows of the beach. The park is popular with open water dive classes, so it can get busy on a weekend.

Name:	**Sund Rock Wreck**
Location:	Sund Rock North Wall, Hood Canal.
Position:	**47° 26.227' N 123° 07.171' W**
Depth:	**30-60'**
Access:	**Shore Dive**, Sund Rock North Wall.
Rating:	**Beginner.**
Currents:	**Negligible.**

History: The *Sund Rock Wreck* was clearly brought in and scuttled for diving purposes. (And very well done I might add.)

Dive Information: The wreck, a 55-foot wooden boat, faces nearly east with the bow on the lower slope. It is deteriorating rapidly but has the form of a west coast wooden fishing boat. You can still explore the holds and see the engine and shaft. The prop is missing, but the rudder is quite impressive. Peering into the forecastle hatch, you will see the ribs of the old boat and a few rockfish that are relieved you are not a ling cod. The tripod mast lies off the port side amidships.

Notes: This is an excellent wreck to explore and to enjoy without the need for a dive boat. You can easily locate her by following the 45-foot depth contour north from the north end of the north wall at Sund Rock (that's a lot of norths young man). A guideline is often run from the wall to the wreck, but it is simple to locate even without the line.

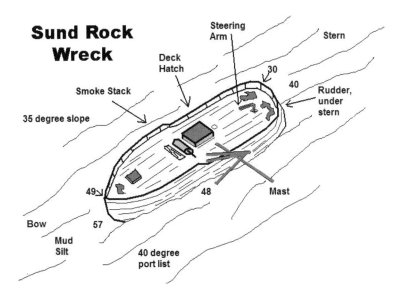

Sund Rock Wreck

Steering Arm

Stern

Deck Hatch

30

40

Smoke Stack

Rudder, under stern

35 degree slope

49

48

Mast

Bow

57

Mud Silt

40 degree port list

You will usually find an orange buoy floating above the wreck, which will help new divers in their navigation. The *Sund Wreck* is large enough to keep you interested for a dive and safe enough to take curious new wreck divers too.

The Sund Rock Marine Preserve at this location is also one of the best dive sites in all of Hood Canal. Stop by Hood Sport 'N Dive in Hoodsport to pay your entry fee (Mr. Sund owns the property). You can park a few feet from the water for one of the easiest and most pleasant shore diving experiences in the Northwest. There are several walls to dive so take the BBQ, make a day of it, and dive them all!

There is also a very small boat located directly out in front of the paid parking area at Sund Rock. It is in about 35 feet of water right next to the mooring buoy used to tie up visiting dive boats.

Cautions: You can get inside this wreck if you aren't careful, but don't. It is too old, and there is really nothing interesting to see other than what is visible through the hatches.

151

Name:	**Taylor Bay Wreck**
Location:	Taylor Bay, Key Peninsula, South Puget Sound.
Position:	**47° 11.041' N 122° 47.075' W**
Depth:	**35-70'**
Access:	**Boat Dive**, ramps at Zittle's Marina 1.5 miles southwest or Boston Harbor 6 miles southwest.
Rating:	**Beginner.**
Currents:	**+20 minutes after Tacoma Narrows North. Significant localized current near high tide.**

History: Often listed as a Surplus Minesweeper, this 168-foot wood-hulled vessel was salvaged on the shore of Taylor Bay and then burned to the waterline. She was then pushed out into the bay to sink. Two conflicting reports list the sinking as 1959 for a wood-hulled sub chaser and 1964 for a minesweeper. Research would indicate that all of the wood-hulled US Naval Sub-chasers and Minesweepers of this length had twin shafts and this wreck only has a single propeller.

Dive Information: The inside of the hull has filled up with sand. It is only about 35 feet deep but is loaded with nudibranchs, rockfish and anemones. Descending along the sides of the hull to the bottom, the forward end of the wreck is deeper than the stern. Peering underneath the wreck, you'll find many ling cod and rockfish hanging out in the "caverns" formed by the curvature of the hull.

Cautions: This location is popular with fishermen and there is often a lot of discarded fishing lures and monofilament line around the wreck. You can easily anchor in the middle of this site, but may foul your anchor when recovering it.

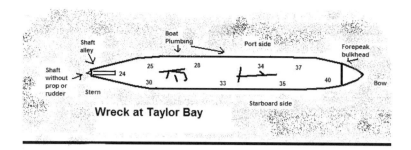

Wreck at Taylor Bay

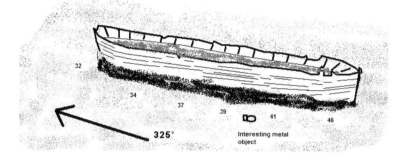

325°   Interesting metal object

Name:	**Taylor Bay Tug**
Location:	Taylor Bay, Key Peninsula, South Puget Sound.
Position:	**47° 11.005' N 122° 46.847' W**
Depth:	**15-35'**
Access:	**Boat Dive,** ramps at Zittle's Marina 1.7 miles southwest or Boston Harbor 6 miles southwest.
Rating:	**Beginner.**
Currents:	**+20 minutes after Tacoma Narrows North.**

Taylor Bay Tug

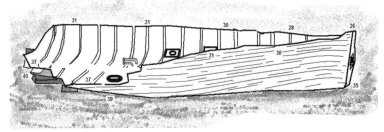

History: The wood-hulled *Taylor Bay Tug* was also salvaged on the shore of Taylor Bay and burned to the waterline. She was then pushed out into the bay to sink near the old Ferry Pilings. This likely happened at about the same time as the other wreck in Taylor Bay. Little else is known about the origin of this shell, which has deteriorated more than the larger *Taylor Bay Wreck*.

Dive Information: This is a comfortable, shallow dive that would make a good second dive site. This wreck seems less affected by current than the larger wreck and is less known to the local fishermen, so may be a safer dive during fishing season. The inside of the hull is only about 20 feet deep and is filled with sand, shells, and nudibranchs. Numerous sculpins, rockfish, and anemones also decorate the ribs of the hull. Descending over the sides of the hull, the bottom averages only 30 feet deep. Peering underneath the wreck, you'll find many sea stars and rockfish hanging out under the curvature of the hull.

Cautions: Other than the occasional jellyfish coming by and raising a welt across your upper lip, this is a pretty benign wreck to dive. It is a good way to spend the remaining air in your tank after diving the larger wreck in Taylor Bay.

Name:	**Tolmie Barges**
Location:	Tolmie State Park, Olympia.
Position:	**47° 07.415' N 122° 46.230' W**
Depth:	**40-50'**
Access:	**Boat Dive or Shore Dive** , ramp at Zittle's Marina 3.5 miles northwest or swim from shore.
Rating:	**Beginner.**
Currents:	**+20 minutes after Tacoma Narrows North.**

History: Three large wooden barges were sunk in front of Tolmie State Park as fish habitat in 1965. Mooring buoys were also placed near the barges for use by boaters.

Dive Information: This is a very pleasant dive (from a boat) that is not current sensitive and is well protected from a southerly wind. All three can be visited in a single dive; although the furthest and largest barge is my favorite (coordinates above).   A white and orange buoy marks the shallower and smaller of the three and is what you crazy swimmers should aim for.

Notes: The muddy bottom offers good anchorage for boats. Just be sure to put out more than 50 feet of scope on your anchor line when anchoring your brand new boat here--but don't ask me how I know that! Scootering all the way out to the barges from shore would be good practice and an interesting challenge.

Cautions: The swim from shore out to the wrecks is more like a marathon (easily 1200 feet). For those that like an aerobic swim, this might be their wreck.

Name:	**Two Pump Chump**
Location:	Friday Harbor, San Juan Islands
Position:	**48° 32.170' N 123° 00.524' W**
Depth:	**40-60'**
Access:	**Boat Dive**, Friday Harbor ramp ½ mile southeast.
Rating:	**Beginner.**
Currents:	**Negligible.**

History: The *Two Pump Chump* was most likely a small, mid-ocean shark and swordfish boat. The net reel, propeller guard, and stern roller on the back deck are indicative of that type of fishery. There are two large hydraulic pumps on board (hence the name of this wreck) and the wheelhouse is intact. This vessel appears to have been sunk many years ago, but is in reasonably good shape.

Dive Information: At around 60 feet long, the *Chump* is lying on its starboard side in 55 feet of water. She rises about 13 feet off the bottom and offers a nice, sheltered dive in the San Juan Islands. A group can take turns discovering interesting niches, valves, rigging, and spots for creatures to hide on the wreck.

Notes: This is a very fun, highly interesting, and easy dive right in the protected waters of Friday Harbor. The *Chump* should be on your list of "must do" dives if you happen to be in the area. This wreck won't last much longer in its present condition, so visit her soon and take care so that other divers can enjoy this dive as well.

Two Pump Chump

Map by JC with sponsorship from Nubluis Bestus, a blockbuster movie about a heroic dog who was very good looking also.
Mapped 06/08

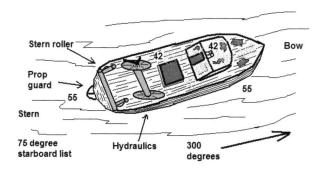

Please do not drop your anchor right on top of this wreck. A few hits from a large boat anchor will be catastrophic to the *Chump's* integrity. Your fellow divers will appreciate your anchoring near her and running a line from the anchor to the wreck for ease of navigation.

Cautions: This site is very close to the main boating channel in Friday Harbor and is not too far away from the Washington State Ferry landing. It would not be a good idea to stray too far away while diving here. There is a lot of boat traffic in the harbor, so be sure to fly a dive flag and leave someone in the boat to help ward off any errant boat captains that decide to get a little too close.

Did you ever get the feeling that they think the red flag with the white stripe means, "come on over and see what is going on?" Given the age and condition of this wreck, penetration is not recommended. Collapse is imminent and you don't want to be inside when your bubbles help it decide to go.

Name:	Tyee
Location:	Commencement Bay, Tacoma
Position:	**47° 17.710' N 122° 25.446' W**
Depth:	**80-120'**
Access:	**Boat Dive**, ramps at Point Defiance 4 miles west or small boats at Dash Point 2.5 miles north.
Rating:	**Advanced, due to depth, very low visibility.**
Currents:	**Negligible.**

History: Beneath the floating breakwater of the Tyee Marina in Tacoma lies a virtual bonanza of wrecks. They were once used as part of the breakwater to protect the boats in the marina. We counted seven barges and three ship hulls lying on the bottom when we ran by with the side scan sonar. Unfortunately, most of those wrecks are off limits to divers with BIG signs that warn you to keep 100 feet away from those future wrecks that make up that floating eyesore.

Dive Information: If you head out away from the marina into the deeper waters to the south, not too far from the barge storage area, you'll find plenty of divable wrecks. My favorite is a large refrigeration ship sitting on a very steep slope that we call the *Tyee*. This ship measures 180 feet long (via sonar), but the stern is actually buried in the silt at about 120 feet deep.

It's a long swim from end to end, but the bow is pretty cool. It extends past the top of the hill, jutting out into green water, which allows divers to swim below the hull with room to spare. An old concrete section from the first Lake Washington Floating Bridge also lies just west of and partially underneath the hull of the refrigeration ship.

Several large cargo holds are easy to drop into and you can still see the refrigeration piping and blowers that once kept the fish frozen on their way to market. There is no superstructure left, and everything in this area is completely covered with several feet of very fine silt from the Puyallup River. Watch your fin technique and have a great dive.

Notes: There are several vessels lying on the bottom in this corner of the bay, including the gas scow *Tyee* (sank in 1927), the motor launch *Arrow* (sank in 1910) and the gas scow *Nome* (stranded in 1929). Sadly, they are slowly disappearing into the silt, making identifying which wreck is which anyone's guess. (Photo shows the bow of the *Quartermaster Wreck*.)

Cautions: This is a busy commercial harbor, so watch out for tugs with barges, ships and other traffic coming in and out of the marinas. The visibility is typically very poor on these wrecks, making navigation difficult. It is easy to stray into areas where you can't make a direct ascent to the surface (like under the barges or breakwater). I would classify this as a very advanced wreck dive even though it really isn't that deep. The blanket of silt is very thick on top of these wrecks which means this dive is not for everyone. It can be a fun dive for the wreck fanatics among us though.

Name:	**War Hawk**
Location:	Mill Point, Discovery Bay
Position:	**48° 00.8708' N 122° 51.4896' W**
Depth:	**25-35'**
Access:	**Boat Dive**, Gardiner Boat Ramp 4 miles north.
Rating:	**Beginner.**
Currents:	**Negligible.**

History: The *War Hawk* is one of the oldest wrecks in our area and is in astonishing condition. She was built in 1855 and was the sister ship to the famous *Flying Cloud*. The last part of her career was carrying wood and timber from the Port Discovery Mill to San Francisco. She had also made the run from New York City to San Francisco, via Cape Horn, ten times. Some of her more ignominious moments were in Coolie trading (Chinese immigrants) and some rather awful years in transporting them to South America to mine guano.

In the early hours of April 12, 1883, while tied up to the dock at the Port Discovery Mill, the *War Hawk* caught fire. After a valiant try to save her she was set adrift to prevent the fire from spreading to the dock and mill. The *War Hawk* drifted a few hundred feet south and settled to the bottom in 35 feet of water.

Dive Information: A very pleasant dive on an amazing bit of history is just a short boat ride away! This Clipper Ship rolled off the shipyard ways more than five years before the Civil War broke out. Now sitting just 35 feet deep on a flat bottom, she is remarkably intact. While you won't see deck planking any more, you will find a good portion of the hull standing proud.

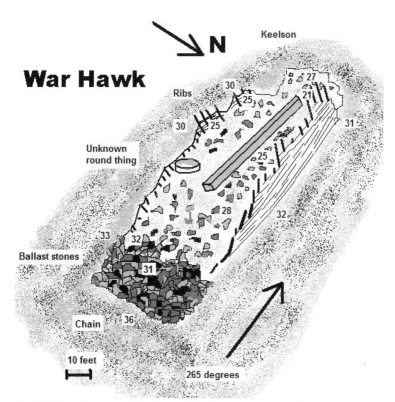

War Hawk

At 193 feet long and 35 feet wide, the *War Hawk*, like many of the Yankee Clippers of her time, was built for speed with a long, narrow hull.

Notes: It is easy to find this wreck using the position on the previous page and a depth sounder. Please do not drop your anchor directly onto this grand old lady. She is much too delicate and could easily be damaged. It is simple to navigate from an anchor that is dropped a few feet away. If anyone can identify what the "unknown round thingy" in the middle is, please let us know (for full credit in the next edition).

Cautions: Ya, um,,, there aren't many dangers here. Be careful anyway. Oh, don't swim under any part of the hull. I knew there was something!

161

Name:	**Warren Wreck**
Location:	Ambulance Point, Crescent Lake
Position:	**48° 03.508' N 123° 52.948' W**
Depth:	**160-170'**
Access:	**Shore Dive**, entry at Meldrim Point.
Rating:	**Technical, due to depth.**

History: The *Warren Wreck* is located in about 170 feet of water off of Ambulance Point in Lake Crescent. It is an amazing dive back into history. Blanch and Russell Warren were returning home from Port Angeles on July 3, 1929, to be with their sons for the 4th of July. They never made it home, disappearing without a trace and leaving a mystery that took nearly 75 years to solve.

Highway 101 was then a treacherous road along the southern shore of Lake Crescent. It was long suspected that the Warrens' car had slid off the road into the lake, but numerous attempts to drag the lake and exploratory dives had failed to turn up their vehicle. The Warren boys, Charles and Frank, were only twelve and fourteen when their parents disappeared. They had a tough life, teased that their parents had run off. Both died tragically without knowing what had really happened to 'Mom' and 'Dad.'

Fast forward to 2001 when Bob Caso, a former diver, kept pestering Dan Pontbraind, a Ranger for the Olympic National Park, to continue the search for the Warrens' 1927 Chevrolet. Evidence gathered in 1929 suggested the accident had occurred at Madrona Point, but there was no "Madrona Point" on any of the maps of the Lake.   A fortunate glance up the cliff near "Meldrim Point" (aka Ambulance Point) from a boat revealed an old Madrona tree hiding among the firs.

The search began in earnest near Ambulance Point (mile marker

162

223) and in 2002 the Park Service Dive Team found the Warrens' 1927 Chevrolet in 170 feet of water just east of the point. Human remains were discovered nearby by John Rawlings in 2004 which DNA testing later proved to be those of Russell Warren.

Dive Information: The *Warren Wreck* sits on a very steep slope with the top of the car downhill. The undercarriage is upslope and is more than half covered with rocks, making the vehicle very hard to spot from above. However, when swimming along at about 165 feet, the wreck is easily located and the clear waters of the lake make this a very rewarding dive.

Notes: The best way to visit this wreck is to go with someone who has been there before. Several groups of local technical divers make annual trips to the lake, making it pretty easy to tag along with an experienced group. There is a good staging area and convenient parking right at "Meldrim Point."

Cautions: Diving the *Warren Wreck* requires a permit from the National Park Service and is just a bit too deep for recreational divers. Watch for cars flying by on Highway 101 while gearing up and boats once you enter the water. Be safe and have a great dive on an interesting bit of Northwest history.

Name: **Western Anchor**

Location: Neah Bay

Position: **48° 22.361' N   124° 37.255' W**

Depth: **20-25'**

Access: **Boat Dive**, ramp at Neah Bay ½ mile southeast.

Rating: **Beginner.**

Currents: **Negligible.**

History: Evidence suggests that this small 35-foot long wreck suffered a fatal fire that sent it to the ocean floor. There is no sign of the bulwarks or any upper deck structure and ample wood remains below the waterline.

The *Western Anchor* looks like a diesel-powered fishing boat with mechanical steering which points to a vintage of more than 50 years ago. The name comes from the location of the wreck in the Western Anchorage area of Neah Bay and can be abbreviated as W.Anker if you like (which can be confused with the term "wanker").

Dive Information: This wreck, like the *Sognefjord*, lies inside of Neah Bay proper which has very limited visibility (typically less than 15 feet). The rudder, steering quadrant, and propeller are located at the stern and are exposed. These features are good examples of the mechanical units that drive and steer a boat. Lying in and around the wreck are some deck equipment and hoses. In the middle you will find the diesel engine along with two fuel tanks on each side. Steel portholes, bilge pumps, and an old steering wheel are lying scattered around on the bottom.

Western Anchor

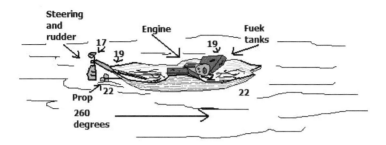

Notes: This is not the most exciting wreck, but it does have some very cool features. When coupled with the *Sognefjord*, this might make a good single tank adventure. Both wrecks are relatively small in size and shallow in depth. The little things are what make this dive fun. It is an excellent beginner dive for people just starting out their wreck diving careers. It is also a good "salvage the day" dive for those wishing for improved weather when they can get out to the much better sites in the open ocean.

Cautions: There is very little to worry about other than sparse boat traffic that a dive flag should fend off. The silt can float up with an errant fin kick, so be sure to drop your anchor a ways off the wreck. This will keep you from damaging what is left of this old fishing boat.

On a steering gear, the rudder quadrant or 'steering quadrant' is the section of the sheave or wheel that is fastened to the rudder head that allows the rudder to turn when the wheel is turned.

Name:	**Wingina (aka Murph)**
Location:	Quartermaster Harbor, Vashon Island
Position:	**47° 21.2144' N 122° 29.2383' W**
Depth:	**3 – 30'**
Access:	**Boat Dive**, ramps at Point Defiance 3 miles south or Gig Harbor 5.5 miles west.
Rating:	**Beginner.**
Currents:	**Moderate.**

History: The *Wingina*, (former medium *Yard Tug 395*) was built in January 1944 in Jacksonville, Florida, by Gibbs Gas Engine Company. She was reclassified as *YTB-395* on May 15, 1944. The tug spent most of her time as part of the Columbia River Group, assisting vessels while stationed out of Astoria, Oregon.

After decommissioning and being resold several times the vessel went through a number of names, ending her days afloat named the *Murph*. She was anchored at her final resting place in Quartermaster Harbor between Vashon and Maury Islands. The *Murph* is a 101-foot long, steel-hulled tug that displaces 260 tons; the single four-blade propeller (nine feet in diameter) is an impressive sight for divers. She was scuttled in October 2007, and now sits upright on the sandy bottom of Quartermaster Harbor in only 30 feet of water.

Dive Information: The wreck lies 850 yards northwest of the red number 2 buoy just off of Manzanita. She is well marked by two large yellow lighted navigational buoys, making it easy to locate and at this shallow depth it is a very relaxed dive. Use caution when approaching the wreck site as the mast of the tug lies only three feet below the surface at low tides.

Wingina

90 degrees

The *Wingina* was obviously stripped before being scuttled. There is really nothing left inside but some rotting furniture. All of the inspection and access hatches are tied open with rope, clearly indicating that the sinking was deliberate.

Notes: The *Wingina* makes a nice second dive after diving the *Quartermaster Wreck* which is only a quarter-mile southeast. Anchor your boat in a safe location and swim to the wreck; it's a very large target that is easily visible from the surface.

This wreck is on the Department of Natural Resources list of derelict vessels and is slated to be floated and removed or salvaged at some point because it is a hazard to navigation. Be sure to dive her before she disappears.

Cautions: Watch out for the large anchor draped over the port aft rail as you make your way around the wreck. It is swings around in the mild current and is a bit disconcerting when you "bump" your head on it. Quartermaster Harbor usually doesn't have a lot of water movement which results in generally poor visibility and fewer invertebrates than those exposed to the currents of the Narrows.

Wreck of the War Hawk

Jefferson Head Minesweeper

Charter Only Wrecks

Name: **Admiral Sampson**

Location: Point No Point.

Depth: **320'**

Access: **Charter.**

Rating: **Technical.**

History: The steel-hulled, luxury passenger liner *Admiral Sampson* was en route from Seattle to Alaska when disaster struck. While passing Point No Point in the fog on August 26, 1914, the bow of the *Princess Victoria* sliced into the side of the *Sampson*, and the cold waters of Puget Sound began to rush in. Both vessels were traveling at a mere three knots, but the damage was severe and the fuel oil on the *Sampson* caught fire forcing the *Victoria* to back away.

The 296-foot long *Admiral Sampson* sank stern first. There were eleven of her 160 passengers still on board along with five members of the crew (including the doomed ship's captain, Zimro Moore) when she met her demise.

Notes: This is an extremely deep wreck located right in the middle of the southbound traffic lane. She is often buffeted by deep currents that run contrary to the calm on the surface. These days the vessel lies in two parts and is one of the most impressive dives in the Pacific Northwest.

Cautions: The only safe way to dive this wreck is from a charter boat. Diving at this depth in high traffic areas requires extensive training, planning, and experience.

Name:	**A.J. Fuller**
Location:	Elliot Bay, Seattle
Depth:	**240'**
Access:	**Charter.**
Rating:	**Technical.**

History: The square-rigged windjammer, *A.J. Fuller* was built in Maine in 1881. This beautiful, 230-foot long ship had just discharged several hundred passengers from Kodiak Island. She was moored to a buoy in Elliott Bay waiting for dock space when she was struck (in heavy fog) by the steamship *Mexico Maru*.

The *Fuller* was heavily laden with cargo from Alaska, including 48,000 cases of canned salmon and 4,000 barrels of salted fish. It took only ten minutes for the majestic ship to sink in 240 feet of cold, dark water. The collision and sinking took place on October 30, 1918, a mere 2000 feet from the west end of Harbor Island.

Notes: Please see the list of technical-friendly dive charter operators located on our web site (northwestwreckdives.com) if you are interested in diving this wreck.

Cautions: Elliot Bay is a very busy commercial harbor, and the *A.J. Fuller* is located in an area controlled by the Coast Guard's Vessel Traffic Service (VTS). The only safe way to dive this wreck is from a charter boat with a professional captain that checks in and clears the dive operations with VTS. Diving wrecks at this depth in high traffic areas requires extensive training, planning, and experience.

Name:	**Bunker Hill**
Location:	Rosario Strait, west of Sares Head
Positions:	48° 25.6612' N 122° 44.6767' W stern
	48° 25.0580' N 122° 44.5353' W bow
Depth:	**280'**
Access:	**Charter**, Washington Park boat ramp is located 5 miles north or charter pick-up in Anacortes.
Rating:	**Technical.**
Currents:	**Burrows Island Light.**

History: The 524-foot long tanker *SS Bunker Hill* had just completed offloading its cargo of bunker oil in Tacoma. She was proceeding north in the Rosario Strait on her way to Anacortes to load more oil at the refinery. On March 7, 1964, while cleaning the empty tanks, something went horribly wrong and the vessel was ripped apart by an explosion. This set the ship on fire which caused the hull to split into two sections and sink in the deep water between Fidalgo and Lopez Islands.

Captain Abraham and four members of his crew died in the fire that consumed the vessel. Rumors persist to this day that the explosion was caused by an old Navy sunken bomb, but it is far more likely (and somewhat common) that the vapors in the cargo tanks were ignited by the Butterworth machine that was used to clean the tanks.

Both the bow and stern sections appear on NOAA charts and are listed as separate wrecks. The 300-foot long forward section includes the superstructure and bridge and is the section generally visited by divers.

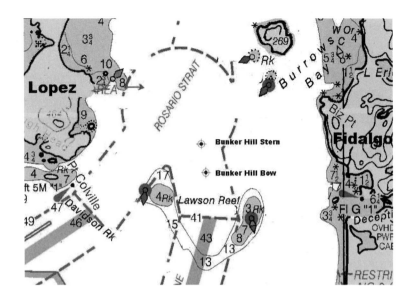

Dive Information: The *Bunker Hill* is a challenging site due to its depth and the location right at the meeting point of two very busy traffic lanes. The best way to visit this wreck is to sign up with one of the local charter operators listed on our web site. With the bottom at nearly 280 feet of depth and the massive propeller and rudder located at 220 feet, good surface support and mild conditions are needed to dive this wreck safely.

Notes: The northern section is lying upside down a little over one half mile north of the larger bow section. The stern of the *Bunker Hill* is located 2.8 miles west of Sares Head on Fidalgo Island. The bow section is located six-tenths of a mile south southwest of the stern.

Cautions: This is a very demanding wreck to dive and should only be attempted by those divers with the right training and experience. Surface support will help fend off the large ships traversing the area. A professional charter captain that maintains constant communication with the U.S. Coast Guard Vessel Traffic Control is your best bet.

Name:	**Coaster**
Location:	Point No Point, near the *Admiral Sampson*.
Depth:	**185'**
Access:	**Charter.**
Rating:	**Technical.**

History: The 140 ton *M/V Coaster* was launched in British Columbia in 1916. The vessel became famous when it collided with the steamship *North Coast* off Point No Point on the night of August 25, 1938. The 94-foot long *Coaster* was heading from Alaska to a Tacoma smelter with 109 tons of gold ore concentrates. The seven-man crew was rescued but the small ship sank to the ocean floor in 185 feet of water and the gold concentrates have never been recovered.

Notes: The *Coaster* broke in two after she sank and now lies in separate pieces that are somewhat difficult to locate due to the rather small size of this wreck. Many divers are a bit under-whelmed by their visits to the *Coaster*. The wreck sits in a high current area that is best to dive during slack on a very small exchange.

Cautions: This hulk is located close to the traffic lanes that are used by the southbound ships coming into Puget Sound. This area is controlled by Puget Sound Vessel Traffic Service (VTS). The safe way to dive her is from a charter boat with a professional captain that checks in and clears the dive operations with VTS. Diving wrecks at this depth in high traffic areas requires extensive training, planning, and experience.

Name: **Dawn**

Location: Lake Washington, Atlantic City

Depth: **120'**

Access: **Charter.**

Rating: **Technical.**

History: The *Dawn* was a wood-hulled, passenger steamer ferry that was built at the Houghton Shipyard in Kirkland in 1914. The 55-foot-long vessel ferried passengers back and forth between Mercer Island and Leschi Park in Seattle. Larger automobile ferries took over the inland routes and forced her out of business. The *Dawn* was scuttled in 1938 one mile east of the Atlantic City Boat Ramp.

Dive Information: The *Dawn* is a pretty, model-like ferry that is one of the best wreck dives at the south end of Lake Washington. Unfortunately, it is also easily damaged and will not stand up well to a lot of traffic and anchoring. We have been asked not to publish the coordinates for this wreck. Our hope is that you will visit this amazing bit of history on one of our local charter boats or with one of the groups of experienced local wreck divers that use soft shot line techniques to dive this wreck.

Notes: Please see the map of the *Dawn* on the next page.

Cautions: Like most of the dives in Lake Washington, diving the *Dawn* is dark, and the low visibility makes it very easy to become disoriented. This can lead to losing both your buddy and the up-line back to the surface. On several dives, I have unknowingly swum into the cabin or covered foredeck. This unwittingly places divers without a direct ascent to the surface, so do be careful.

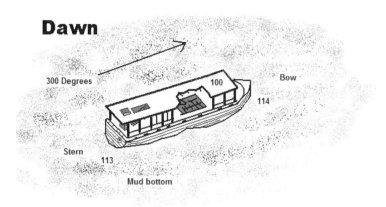

Dawn

300 Degrees

100

Bow

114

Stern
113

Mud bottom

Forepeak of the forward deck cover of the Ferry Dawn.

Name:	**Governor**
Location:	Point Wilson, Admiralty Inlet
Position:	**48° 09.3822' N 122° 45.0035' W**
Depth:	**240'**
Access:	**Boat Dive**, Port Townsend 4 miles southwest or charter out of Anacortes.
Rating:	**Technical.**
Currents:	**Point Wilson.**

History: The 392-foot long steam powered ocean liner *Governor* was built in Camden, New Jersey in 1907. She carried 540 passengers and 120 crew members at a pleasant 15 knots. She was operating on a run from San Francisco to Seattle. She made a brief stop in Victoria on April Fool's Day in 1921 and then collided with the *West Hartland*, sinking off of Point Wilson, near Port Townsend.

The *Governor* has long piqued the interest of many local divers and salvage companies. There have been numerous attempts over the years to locate the casino safe on board the ship that is reported to contain gold. The value of this gold has been hyped to epic proportions, but the howling currents and dangerous diving conditions have forced most would-be treasure hunters to quickly abandon their search for the elusive safe.

Dive Information: The only way to visit the *Governor* is to join one of the charters that dive this deep wreck which is located right in the middle of one of our busiest shipping lanes. A professional captain will help keep you safe by maintaining constant contact with USCG Vessel Traffic Control. This wreck it typically available for diving about one weekend per year.

Name:	**Multnomah**
Location:	Elliot Bay, Seattle
Depth:	**270'**
Access:	**Charter.**
Rating:	**Technical.**

History: The old Columbia River stern wheeler, *Multnomah* was working the Olympia – Seattle run on October 28, 1911. She had stopped to pick up a load of cattle and was proceeding into Elliott Bay to discharge the cargo when she was rammed by the steamer *Iroquois* in heavy fog. The 143-foot long vessel sank in 270 feet of water with the terrified livestock still chained to the decks of the old steamer.

Notes: Like the nearby *A.J. Fuller*, this wreck is best to dive from one of our local charter operators. In the past, divers have reported that the old stern wheeler is sitting upright on the bottom and that the skeletons of the long dead cattle and horses are chained in place. That makes for a rather spooky dive in the cold dark waters of Elliott Bay.

Cautions: This wreck is located in a very busy commercial area controlled by the Coast Guard's Vessel Traffic Service (VTS). The only safe way to dive this wreck is from a charter boat with a professional captain that checks in and clears the dive operations with VTS. Diving wrecks at this depth, in high traffic areas, requires extensive training, planning, and experience.

Name:	**YMS Minesweepers**
Location:	Lake Washington, Seattle
Depth:	**200'**
Access:	**Charter.**
Rating:	**Technical.**

History: Three YMS class minesweepers lie where they were scuttled in the middle of the northern part of Lake Washington. The *YMS-416* was built in Cleveland, Ohio, in 1944 and was burned and sunk off of Houghton in 1952. This vessel is in the worst shape of the three wrecks and is often called the *Healy*.

The *YMS-359* was built in 1943 in New York, served through WWII and was sold to a private individual in 1948. Rumor has it that restoration plans lacked funding and the *YMS-359* suffered from a fire so was taken out to the middle of the lake and sunk.

The most recently discovered YMS class minesweeper is located very near the other two in 200 feet of water. There are no numbers on the bow, so positive identification has not been made. We tend to refer to her as *YMS #3*. She is the best preserved of the bunch and makes for an awesome dive.

Notes: The coordinates for the *Healy* are publicly available and several of our recommended charters will take you there. These minesweepers were 136-feet long wood-hulled vessels with twin screws that displaced about 270 tons.

Cautions: A 200-foot deep dive in the cold, dark waters of Lake Washington requires a lot of training and experience. Be sure to work up to these dives by tackling some of the shallower dives first.

Jefferson Head Minesweeper.

Boiler of the S.S. Burton.

Appendices

Emergency Dive Information

Divers Alert Network (DAN) (919) 684-8111

Coast Guard

Rescue Center Washington & Oregon (206) 220-7001

Tacoma (800) 982-2564

Port Angeles (360) 417-5913

Port Townsend (360) 385-3070

Neah Bay (360) 645-2195

Bellingham (360) 752-2722

Virginia Mason Hospital

Emergency Room (206) 583-6433

Hyperbaric Unit 24-Hour Consultation (206) 583-6543

British Columbia

Rescue Center (Victoria) (800) 567-5111

EMERGENCY RADIO FREQUENCIES

U.S. Coast Guard VHF Channel 16

Canadian Coast Guard VHF Channel 16

RECOMPRESSION CHAMBERS

British Columbia

Fleet Diving Unit Pacific, Victoria (250) 363-2379

Vancouver General Hospital, Vancouver (604) 875-4111

Oregon

Providence Hospital, Portland (503) 230-6061

Washington

Virginia Mason Hospital, Seattle (206) 583-6543

Diver's Institute of Technology, Seattle (206) 783-5543

Fairchild AFB, Spokane (E.R.)(509) 247-5661
(Chamber)(509) 247-5406

U.S. Naval Station, Keyport (360) 396-2552 (24 hrs)
(360) 296-2551

Why we dive Wrecks

The story of the Golden Coin.

Some things cannot be made to change.

In a land not far away, and not unlike the land you see outside, there is a harbor called Quartermaster Harbor. The bay changes little, with a slow influx of tide and wind that wanders in and drifts out in the same way year after year.

One fine day, while meandering through the water, a boat full of divers came to Quartermaster Harbor. One of them, Scott, had discovered a shipwreck and they were returning to the depths to introduce her to a new admirer, Jeff.

The water was murky, but the hull rose off of the bottom like a mountain emerging through the fog. One could only see the dark shape above and the wooden planks ahead. As they swam over her railings and onto the deck, the glory of the wreck swept over them. Here was a broken mast, a beautiful wooden hull, a sweeping bow and rounded stern. You could almost hear the ghostly waves echoing against the old timbers. How old is this wreck? Where did it come from? How did it sink? Who was the last to walk this deck?

Looking into the dark reaches of the boat they spotted a bag lying in the corner of a shelf deep inside the bow. It was a small canvas bag and it was out of reach, barely. They left it, then returned. They reached, but couldn't get it. So they left it, and returned. The bag kept bringing them back to that hatch. With an old branch they moved it closer, but it was still out of reach. Barely. Scott then made a contortioned effort and spun in four directions at once. He had snagged the bag by the hemp drawstring.

The contents of the bag were emptied on the deck and the silt was allowed to settle. Inside were bits of metal and rust. The divers left it, and then returned.

Just off to one side, buried in rusted grime and silt was a rounded shape. Jeff grabbed it eagerly and began to scrap the rust away. Right before his eyes, like magic, appeared a coin! A shiny gold coin! After a high-five, (maybe more than one high-five), they proceeded to the anchor line, and up.

The three minute safety stop seemed like nine hours, eleven minutes and 36 seconds. Every couple of seconds Jeff checked his coin pocket to make sure it was still zipped. The coin seemed to have an effect on him, making him return to it, his Precious!

The divers arrived safely on the surface and crawled back onto the boat, stripping off gear as quickly as they possibly could. Then the gloves came off and the zippered pocket was opened, and with great relief they both saw the precious golden shine from inside the coin pocket.

A gold coin could be the find of a lifetime, a relic from the days of yore. They both peered at the coin as the grime was washed away, scrape by scrape. Then the lettering began to appear. Maybe something in Spanish? Perhaps U.S. Currency? The first letters they saw were GOD. In God we trust? No, Godfa.... Then they flipped it over to see the letters CASH! What a great word, they thought with glee! But glee never lasts, especially when the next scrape reveals NO CASH VALUE.... In a near panic, they turn the coin over and in big bold letters it read GODFATHERS PIZZA GAMING TOKEN.

Some things can't be made into change, especially stuff that is of no cash value.

Searching with a depth sounder and GPS

You can find an incredible amount of information about a dive site with a GPS unit and a depth sounder (and a boat, of course). Once you have acquired a target or selected an area to search, you should set your perimeter. Make your search perimeter a bit wider than your target area, which gives you time to realign for each search pass. You need to be familiar with your fish finder and what area it covers. The search angle is constant, but the area it searches changes depending on depth.

It is much easier to do this effectively with two people. One should drive the boat and keep a very precise course and the other can watch the sounder carefully. Make notes, plot waypoints and stay your course until you have made a full pass or completed your entire search area.

The most common mistake is getting bored and quitting. The second is to see a bottom feature and quit your search pattern early because you "know you have found it." Early in my career I was sure that I had "found a wreck." It turned out to be a rock. So I looked some more. Since I hadn't bothered to set a waypoint, I eventually "found it" again. I jumped in for a second dive, only to discover that it was the same rock and my anchor had landed only three feet from where it was the first time (I could still see the dent in the sand where it hit on the first go-round). I eventually completed my pattern and found the wreck I was looking for just a few hundred feet away.

Take your time; be thorough and know that not every search yields treasure. Trial and error has taught us that a failure to find something is successful in eliminating that area from further searches. Stay positive; the good stuff is out there.

How to Draw a Dive Map

Be prepared to write down the information you need during your dive. Use a slate or wet notes and jot down the important information right away. Some of the information that you may need is:

Depths
Compass bearings
Slopes/angles
Bottom composition
GPS position

Try to get the scale of your map and all of the features in your notes. If there is a change in depth, take ample depth information. I use a circle around a depth to indicate the top of some feature and no circle means the bottom depth in my notes.

When you hit the surface, review your notes and add any additional information that might be necessary.

At home, select your perspective and draw your map. It can be hours later or the next day. You don't have to be an artist. You just have to convey the information on your map to your audience in a readable way. Practice will make you a better cartographer. After one or two maps, you will no doubt surpass my meager drawing abilities if you have any skill at all.

Don't forget to show your map to your dive buddies. They will provide invaluable feedback, including the, "didn't you see the large anchor sitting out in plain sight?" Doh!

Vessel Traffic Control

"*Seattle Traffic*," Vessel Traffic Service (VTS) Puget Sound is the U.S. Coast Guard section that controls commercial shipping traffic in the region. Divers operating in or around busy harbors and the areas controlled by VTS should check in prior to beginning dive operations and should also notify Seattle Traffic when dive operations are completed.

The best way to notify VTS is to call the Vessel Traffic Service Watchstander at **(206) 217-6152** immediately prior to commencing dive operations and upon completion of operations. Prudent boat captains will also monitor the VTS channel for their region so they know what to expect for commercial vessel movements in their area. The designated VTS channels are:

Channel Designation: Ch 14 (156.700 MHz)
Monitoring Area: The navigable waters of Puget Sound, Hood Canal and adjacent waters south of a line connecting Marrowstone Point and Lagoon Point in Admiralty Inlet and south of a line drawn due east from the southernmost tip of Possession Point on Whidbey Island to the shoreline.

Channel Designation: Ch 5A (156.250 MHz)
Monitoring Area: The navigable waters of the Strait of Juan de Fuca east of 124° 40' W, excluding the waters in the central portion of the Strait of Juan de Fuca north and east of Race Rocks; the navigable waters of the Strait of Georgia east of 122° 52' W.; the San Juan Island Archipelago, Rosario Strait, Bellingham Bay; Admiralty Inlet north of a line connecting Marrowstone Point and Lagoon Point and all waters east of Whidbey Island north of a line drawn due east from the southernmost tip of Possession Point on Whidbey Island to the shoreline.

Additional phone numbers for Seattle Traffic are: (206) 217-6151, 6050, 6052.

Boaters are requested to clear Vessel Traffic lanes as quickly as possible. The rules of the road require that any vessel less than 20 meters in length shall not impede the passage of a vessel which can safely navigate only within a narrow channel. Do not cause a grounding or put your life at risk by thinking a big ship can get out of your way. It is much more practical to avoid large ships and to pass them astern whenever possible.

GPS Data Conversions

If you need to convert our coordinates to decimal degrees, simply divide the minutes by 60 and add them to the degrees to get decimal degrees:

47° 37.2285' N = 47.620475° N
(divide 37.2285' by 60 to get 0.62047° and add to 47°)

If you need to convert the coordinates to degrees, minutes and seconds (dd° mm' ss") then you would take the decimal portion of the decimal minutes, and multiply by 60 to determine the number of seconds:

47° 37.2285' N = 47° 37' 13.71" N
(multiply 0.2285' by 60 to determine the number of seconds)

In the majority of GPS units on the market, you can simply enter the coordinates in any format, and it will convert them for you.

Additional Wreck Maps

Chris Craft

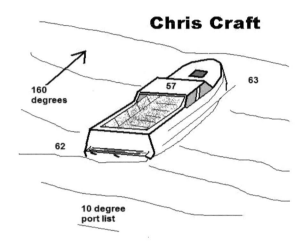

160 degrees

57

63

62

10 degree
port list

Steilacoom Marina Wreck, page 146

Diamond Girl

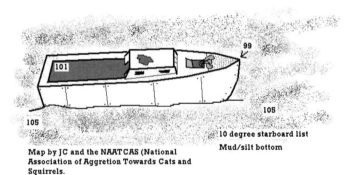

101

99

105

105

10 degree starboard list

Mud/silt bottom

Map by JC and the NAATCAS (National
Association of Aggretion Towards Cats and
Squirrels.

Diamond Girl, page 66

Hatch

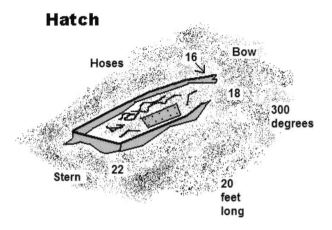

Hoses

16

Bow

18

300 degrees

Stern

22

20 feet long

Steilacoom Marina Wreck, page 146

Wreck Map
Horizontal Barge-Shilshole

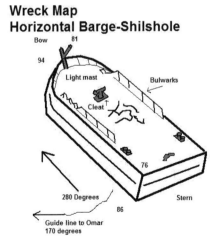

Bow   81

94

Light mast

Bulwarks

Cleat

76

280 Degrees

Stern

86

Guide line to Omar
170 degrees

Shilshole Barges, page 136

Quartermaster Wreck

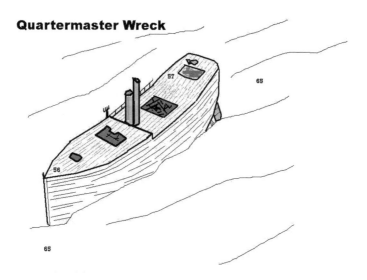

Quartermaster Wreck, page 124

Puget Girl

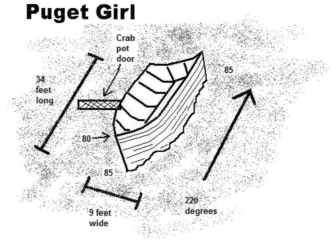

Puget Girl, page 122

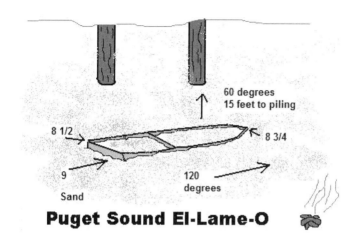

Puget Sound El-Lame-O, page 123

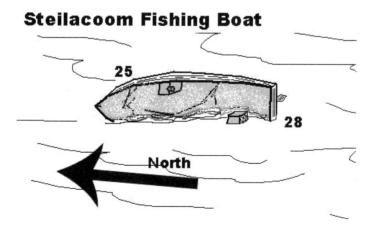

Steilacoom Marina Wreck, page 146

Glossary

Abaft: Toward the Stern.

Access Hatch: An entry place.

Adrift: Afloat and unattached.

Advanced: A diver who has multiple dives in numerous locations who is capable in all aspects of Recreational Diving.

A-Frame: A triangular support truss.

Aft: Back end of a boat.

Aground: When a boat hits the rocks, beach, reef or bottom.

Air Receiver: An air storage device for low pressure compressed air.

Algal Bloom: Sudden plankton or algae growth.

Alpha: A nautical flag consisting of a notched flag with blue and white colors.

Amidships: The center of the vessel.

Anchor: A device designed to slow or stop a vessel drifting.

Anchorage: A place where an anchor will hold well.

Artificial Reef: A man made structure that enables sealife to inhabit where they could not before.

Astern: Toward the back.

Barge: A powerless vessel meant to be towed.

Bark: A sailing vessel rigged with fore and aft sails on the aft mast and square sails on the other masts.

Beam: Width at widest point.

Bearing: Horizontal line of direction or direction of travel.

Beginner: A new diver still acquiring experience in current, navigation, buoyancy, and basic diving skills.

Bilge: Inside bottom of the boat.

Bitt: Posts mounted in a ship for fastening rope, chain, or cable to.

Block: A pulley enclosure.

Boiler: A water storage and heating system used to produce steam.

Boiler Tubes: The tubes running through the boiler that increase the surface area, making it more effective in heating water inside.

Boom: A horizontal mast used for movement of cargo on a vessel.

Bow: The pointed end of a boat. The front.

Bowsprit: The boom-like projection from the bow in front of the prow.

Breakwater: Structure for protecting a beach or harbor.

Bridge: Where the captain drives the boat.

Bulkhead: A wall on a ship.

Bulwarks: The solid railings above the deck.

Bunker Oil: Low grade oil used by bulk carriers as fuel.

Butterworth: An automated tank-cleaning machine similar to a lawn sprinkler.

Cabin: Quarters for the crew, passengers, or cargo.

Capsized: Upside down, exposing the keel.

Capstan: A rotating hub to wrap line around creating pulling friction.

Cleat: A device used to secure line, chain, or cable.

Clipper Ship: A sailing vessel built for speed.

Coastal Motorship: An open ocean ship that plies local waters in trade routes without crossing oceans.

Cockpit: Where the pilot sits to drive a plane.

Compass Bearing: The degree heading you are working with.

Control Cabin: Small enclosure where an operator sits to operate a machine.

Current: Direction and speed of moving water.

Cutlass Bearing: The stern bearing at the end of the keel.

Deck: Horizontal surfaces on vessels.

Decompression: A diving term for exceeding the recreational diving limits and passing the safe limit for a normal ascent.

Degaussing: A method of neutralizing a magnetic field.

Derrick: A lifting device comprised of a high pole and a boom.

Doghouse: A small ventilation structure on a ship resembling a tiny house.

Dolphin: Numerous pilings driven into the seabed in a circular fashion.

Draft: Floating depth of a vessel.

Drift: Allowing current to move you.

Ebb: Outgoing tide.

El-Lame-O: Scubanese for "run, save yourself."

Entanglement Hazard: Any objects which can inhibit a diver's free movement.

Fantail: The rounded stern.

Fastline Jib: The small boom projecting from the end of a crane that handles only light loads from the fast line.

Fathom: Nautical term for 6 feet.

Figurehead: A symbolic image at the bow of a ship.

Fire Bricks: Insulating bricks that provide ballast in the bilge as well as heat protection to the hull and heat retention in the boiler.

Flocculated: Forming cloudy masses.

Flood: Incoming tide.

Flotsam: Floating junk, scum and goo.

Flying Bridge: A protected but uncovered bridge on top of the wheelhouse.

Fore Deck: A deck in front of the bridge.

Forecastle: Quarters or enclosed area in the bow.

Foundered: To fill with water and sink.

GPS: Global Positioning System

Gudgeons: A socket for a hinge.

Guy Wires: Stabilizing stays for raised masts and derricks.

Hatch: A horizontal entry door.

Hawse Holes: A hole in the ship for chain or line to pass through.

Hold: Interior of the ship, generally for cargo.

HP: Horse power.

Hull: Shell framework of the boat.

Intermediate: Divers who have considerable skill in buoyancy, night diving, deep diving, current and navigation, but have not yet mastered them.

Jib: The lattice structure attached to the end of a crane boom.

Jigging: Jerking a line/bait up and down to attract fish.

Keel: Central structure of a hull.

Keelson: Structure immediately above the keel.

Kingpost: Freestanding mast used for cargo movement.

Launch: Small utility boat carried on a larger craft.

Line: Rope.

List: A vessel's angle of lean, port and starboard.

Macro: Photographing the small things.

Magnetic: Direction on a compass. Most charts use true north which must be converted to magnetic before navigating by compass.

Manitowac: A manufacturer of cranes.

Mast: A vertical pole on a ship that supports rigging.

Mast Boss: A box attached to the keel that holds a mast.

Moor: To tie up a boat.

Mosquito Fleet: The small vessel ferry system in Washington State before the larger car carrying system was used.
Moused: Pounding of the end of a pin to swell it.

Nautical Mile: A mile based on 60 miles per degree of latitude. About 1.15 miles.
Net Reel: A spool designed to hold a net.
NOAA: National Oceanographic Atmospheric Administration.

Ocean Liner: A large passenger-carrying ship.

Pendant: Hanging or suspended wire rigging.
Pier: Dock.
Pilothouse: The bridge of a ship.
Pontoons: A round solid floatation device.
Port: Left side of a boat. A harbor.
Portholes: Boat windows.
Pratt and Whitney: Engine manufacturers.
Propeller Guard: A shroud around a prop to keep items from wrapping onto the shaft.
Propellers: Propulsion equipment resembling a fan blade.
Pullmaster: A brand name of a heavy lifting winch.

Radar: A transmitter and receiver of radio signals that determines objects around a vessel's position.
Recreational Diving Limit: Most certifying agencies teaching basic SCUBA regard this as 130 feet of water or less.
Reduction Gear: A boat's transmission.
Ribs: Hull support members running side to side on a ship.
Rigging: A system of masts and lines.
Rode: An anchor shot line.
Rudder: The steering armature on a vessel.
Rudder Post: The shaft that holds the rudder.

Sail: A canvas sheet that transfers air movement to ship energy.
Sampson Post: Strong vertical posts to support a ship's

windlass.

Scow: A flat bottomed vessel.

Scuttle: To sink intentionally.

Shackle: A metal connection device comprising of a ring and pin.

Shaft: A driveline.

Sheave: A pulley for hoisting or hauling with a grooved ring.

Shipping Lane: Designated directional areas for large ship traffic.

Shot Line: Weight and a line.

Side Scan Sonar: Electronic searching device that projects images from the side of the boat not beneath.

Silt: Light material that can be stirred up easily on the bottom.

Slack: A point of no tidal currents.

Slip: A boat parking place.

Smokestack: An exhaust funnel.

Square Rigged: A sailing ship that utilizes square sails on spars.

Stanchion: Vertical posts that support lines and rigging.

Starboard: Right side of the boat.

Stay: Rigging running fore and aft.

Steam Engine: A motor powered by pressurized steam.

Steering Pulley: Mechanical steering gearing.

Steering Quadrant: A rounded gear that transfers a turn of the wheel to rudder movement.

Stern: The back of a boat.

Stern Tube: The tube under the hull that holds the tailshaft.

Superstructure: The above deck inhabited quarters.

Tailshaft: The segment of the shaft that protrudes through the hull.

Technical: Diving beyond recreational limits including decompression, penetration, and deep dives.

Three Minute Safety Stop: A standard safety measure

recommended at 15 feet during the close of each dive.

Tidal Exchange: The rise and fall of tidal flow.

Timber: Wood frames in a ship.

Traffic Separation Scheme: A USCG plan to allow free flow and safe passage of large vessel traffic in crowded areas.

Tug: A vessel made for towing, pushing or hauling by other methods.

Twin Screw: A two propeller craft.

Unknown Round Thingy: If you can figure it out on the Warhawk, we would really like to know.

USCG: United States Coast Guard.

VTS: Vessel Traffic Separation

Waterline: Float line of water on the hull.

Wee Wreck: Small and inconsequential wreck.

Wheelhouse: The bridge of a boat.

Winch: A mechanical hoist.

Windlass: A device for hauling or hoisting.

Wing Wall: A line of protective pilings in a docking area.

Index

Quartermaster Wreck

About the Authors

Jeff Carr

I was born and raised in Oregon and am from the small town of Newport on the central coast. It is there that I began my dive career with the help from my friend Donny Richcreek. He funded my classes to avoid further questioning from me about diving and was good enough to take me along with him for my first 200 dives.

From Newport I found my way to Alaska in the commercial fishing industry from 1985 to 1995. I began my career on the *Royal Quarry* working for Steve Calhoun (featured in the book Working on the Edge by Spike Walker). From there I worked on a joint venture fishery with the Russians on the vessel *Gold Rush*. I finally finished my career on the *Alaska Trojan* working for Dave Capri.

After leaving Alaska, I enrolled at Lane Community College and later, the University of Oregon. I graduated from the U of O in December of 2000 with a Bachelors degree in business marketing. During my time in Eugene, I began my diving career in earnest. In 1997 I received my Divemaster certification and in 1998 I became an instructor for Eugene Skin Divers Supply. I worked for Mike Hollingshead as an instructor until 2002.

I moved to Washington in the fall of 2002 and began my career in the timber industry with Washington Alder, where I work to this day. I am living in Centralia, Washington and only a short distance from south Puget Sound.

I met Scott and Janet in Olympia in 2005 at the Kelp Krawlers Dive Club and quickly realized that I was only the second most obsessive wreck geek that I knew. We began our book project in 2007; and one day in the summer of 2008, we realized that we would never, ever be done with it. When you read this, it is likely that we are out looking for more wrecks.

Jeff's boat, the "Spotted Weasel".

Scott Boyd

Growing up in Washington State, Scott began his love of the ocean at a young age when his family moved to Hammersley Inlet in Mason County. He later ran off to Florida to pursue a Bachelor of Science degree in Ocean Engineering from Florida Institute of Technology. Scott then went to work in the "oil field" as a captain of an off-shore drilling rig while Jeff was playing "Deadliest Catch" in the Bering Sea. His oil-field days lasted fourteen years taking him on many adventures around the world working in various oceans. When he came to his senses and began a "normal" job in the Northwest, Scott felt that something was missing so he took up diving.

Scott also has a passion for underwater photography. After diving a few wrecks in Canada, his quest for new adventures led him to Truk Lagoon. Seeing the living WWII history woke up a fascination for wreck diving. This led to more exploration and adventures in caves and wrecks around the world.

Scott and Jeff were destined to meet--the "old roughneck" and the young crab fisherman. After Jeff's presentation on Great Lakes Wrecks, they have been fast friends and wreck junkies ever since. (Janet says that Scott has been doing plenty of diving, but the house seems to be falling apart around her due to a lack of maintenance--I really don't know what she means!)

Currently, Scott's career entails fixing computer systems that misbehave. He also keeps busy with several side jobs. These include underwater pier inspections, professional photography, webmaster, computer forensics and boat captain. For more information about Scott be sure to check out his website at boydski.com and see some of his beautiful underwater photos.

Scott's Boat, the "Dive Bum"

The authors hope to see you out on the water soon. If you happen to see the *Dive Bum* or *Spotted Weasel* stop by and say hello! If we are cruising around very slowly, we're probably running the side-scan and looking for our next wreck.